Contents

ACKNOWLEDGMENTS

My thanks to the planning committee for IRA's Seventh World Congress on Reading and to all those who served as speakers and chairpersons and to those who participated as listeners and discussants. Only a small portion of the excellence displayed on that program is reflected in the published papers.

Much of the success of the Congress was due to IRA's extraordinary staff whose standards of excellence remained resolute in the face of lost luggage and the sometimes equally traumatic complexities of running a major convention.

My deep appreciation is extended to Faye R. Branca, IRA Professional Publications Editor, whose expertise and assistance in putting these volumes together proved invaluable.

DSS

iv

Foreword

The role of the family as partner to the school in the development of reading success has been largely ignored in many places. In recent years, the International Reading Association has renewed its effort to enlist parent involvement in the reading development of their children through the work of the Parents and Reading Committee. As a consequence, the Association has published a variety of new materials for parents. Special sessions bringing parents and teachers together are featured at the Association's local, state, national, and international meetings. At the 1980 annual IRA convention in St. Louis, over 2500 parents were in attendance at a parents and reading session. Over 200 reading teachers and supervisors attended a two-day preconvention institute concerned with ways of more directly involving parents as partners in helping children learn to read.

Regardless of culture, political persuasion, or geographic location, parents share a common interest in the well-being of their children. Most of us would like to believe that literacy is universally recognized as a desirable, if not an essential, component to a satisfying life. However, the role of literacy in relation to well-being varies widely in various parts of the world. In developing countries with large percentages of illiterate and rural peoples, literacy development by itself is not seen by the people as a useful means of solving their daily problems. It has been demonstrated, however, that the value of literacy increases as development in a country takes place on a broader basis. In the process, significant changes of attitude must take place on the part of parents and governmental officials alike. Recently, while working in a developing country, on several occasions I was told by influential people that it was far better for young boys ages seven to eleven to work in small factories than to go to school. Parents agreed and could not resist the extra income their children's labor provided at the time. They did not think about the reality that as their children matured they would have to leave the factories and would face meager lives as illiterate, unskilled workers. As a consequence, while the number of literate people in the world increases somewhat, the proportion decreases as the rate of population increase exceeds literacy development.

Fortunately, examples exist where this pattern is changing. As development takes place, higher level skills become increasingly important and increasingly rewarded. Parents who are part of the early development begin to value education for their children more highly. New traditions and new patterns develop. National planning increases resources for education. Teacher education is expanded and the years of compulsory school attendance are increased. Literacy development, then, is determined by economics and politics first, and by family considerations second.

This volume in effect assumes that development is taking place and that political forces are providing basic support for education. In such a situation, the family can be both an important force in the educational development of a nation and an important complement to the school. Prime examples of this can be found in the markets of developing nations where parents are often seen tutoring their children, encouraging them to read, and allowing them to participate in the family enterprise at an early age.

The timeliness of this monograph is obvious. If real progress is to be made toward achieving universal literacy, the home must be involved as well as the school. It is hoped that the series of which this volume is a part represents but the first step of the International Reading Association in encouraging and supporting a worldwide partnership of home and school in combating illiteracy.

Leo Fay
Indiana University

"A planet doesn't explode of itself," said drily
The Martian astronomer, gazing off into the air—
"That they were able to do it is proof that highly
Intelligent beings must have been living there."*
—John Hall Wheelock

Introduction

Nations of the world today are beset by problems that seem almost insurmountable. Some of the most obvious are exploding populations, overcrowded cities, air and water pollution, underdeveloped resources, diseases, droughts, floods, earthquakes, starvation, human oppression, power-mad dictators, greedy industrial leaders, self-serving educators and governmental leaders, wars, and the threat of nuclear destruction. But things have been worse. Much worse!

The millenia, centuries, and decades of the past record a history of horror. Only a few thousand years ago it was possible for one whole nation of people to be made the slaves of another nation. Less than two thousand years ago some of the most civilized people in the world found it highly entertaining to watch other human beings being shredded and devoured by hungry wild animals because they deviated in their religious views.

Ten or fifteen centuries ago bands of nomads, boatloads of adventurers, and clans of farmer-warriors regularly pillaged each other, feeling nothing but pleasure in the bloody decimation of the neighboring peoples they robbed. And only two or three centuries ago the tribes on a couple of continents still were capturing their nearby enemies and selling them into lives of subhuman slavery.

Although life had improved greatly, five decades ago one demented monster was able to exploit the frustrations of his people and mislead them in an effort to conquer a large portion of the world and to exterminate a whole ethnic popula-

*"Earth," from *The Gardener and Other Poems* by John Hall Wheelock. Copyright 1961 by John Hall Wheelock. Used by permission of Charles Scribner's Sons.

tion. A quick look at history reveals hundreds of other examples of man's systematic inhumanity to man through the ages.

Today we still have a number of oppressive rulers and a host of criminals, but most people throughout the world do not have to mount a twenty-four hour guard to protect themselves from marauding neighbor tribes. Descendants of former slave families on several continents sometimes may suffer some painful discrimination, but usually they enjoy full citizenship and their lives certainly are not sacrificed at the whim of unfeeling masters. Most of us in all countries have to dig deeply into our pockets to pay taxes for public services, but normally we do not have to fear that all of our earnings will be confiscated by some feudal playboy.

We still fight heart disease and cancer, but we do not worry much about the terrible plagues that wiped out whole communities in the past. We still have hunger, but we also have mechanization that provides food for billions more people than was possible only fifty years ago.

Our progress in improving human conditions on this planet during the past two decades has been nothing less than phenomenal. A major reason is increased literacy.

Literacy has helped to spread the ethical values of the great religions of the world. Consequently, we have progressed from the point a few decades ago when suspected witches were burned at the stake to the point where in some countries people object to the execution of the worst type of murderer. In one overpopulated Asian country, rats are permitted to eat a large portion of the needed food supply simply because the people are too kind to kill the rodents.

Literacy has begun to make people of different lands aware of their human brotherhood so that they often have compassion instead of hate for those needy persons who are ethnically different. Literacy has made it possible to transmit the world's scientific knowledge and to multiply it repeatedly to facilitate communication among peoples and to increase production of the goods needed by all.

The list of local and world problems that we still face, however, shows that the campaign for worldwide literacy has not yet been won. Increased literacy could help to solve some of the remaining problems. Further communication is needed

2

to instill more human idealism, creativity, and habits of perceptive living.

The job is too massive for the schools alone. Because education is a social service instead of the production of a salable product, it is never funded adequately. Consequently, literacy objectives can be fulfilled only by involving parents and volunteers in activities that support the efforts of teachers. If we do not learn how to utilize families in developing literacy today, it is quite possible that the world will explode tomorrow.

HWS

Research Summary: Family Contributions to Reading Attainment

Harry W. Sartain
University of Pittsburgh
Pittsburgh, Pennsylvania
United States of America

After analyzing the correlations of pupil achievement scores with academic aptitude estimates, socioeconomic factors, and instructional factors, McDonald (27) concluded that no more than 36 percent of learning can be attributed to school teaching efforts. If the other two-thirds of a child's knowledge is gained from the home and community, it seems essential for educators to capitalize on family resources in developing reading skills.

Chomsky (6) identified five specific stages of early language development and observed that the rapidity with which children grow through these stages is determined by the socioeconomic status and the reading interests of the children and their parents. Therefore, the quality of home and community experiences during the early years is crucial for children's future educational success. In most countries of the world, however, the school has little influence on what children learn during their first five or six years when they are attaining the understandings and language skills necessary as a foundation for successfully beginning reading. And everywhere— especially in developing countries such as Iran (36) and Malaysia (30)—schools constantly are short of resources to accomplish all they want to do to advance reading.

Traditionally in most countries, schools have been slow to recognize, nurture, and systematically capitalize upon family resources to enhance children's preschool and continuing education, because educators have doubted that families were capable of making valuable contributions. In Japan and Finland, parents usually give children a "head start" before they enter school. Parents elsewhere have become increasingly aggressive in their desires to influence educational programs. In *Education by Choice: The Case for Family Control,* Coons and Sugarman *(10)* argue strongly that parents have the competence for choosing the types of education most suitable for their children. They feel that parents have a greater right than school personnel to make decisions affecting their children, because each individual is different and parents are more concerned about each one than is the school. In Coons' and Sugarman's words:

> Whatever their reasons, modern parents are likely to accord their children the full measure of attention lavished on other values and valuables for which they have been prepared to sacrifice . . . . There is no reason to treat as mere sentiment the human perception that children by and large are loved more by parents than by crossing guards, scoutmasters, welfare workers, and teachers . . ." (p. 56).

Homes of Good and Poor Readers

In learning to read and in attaining favorable attitudes about academic endeavors, children are affected by both the stimulating experiences and the social-emotional climates in their homes.

Family Stimulation

Children who become successful readers usually enter school with an extensive background of experiences that has helped them attain concepts and the vocabulary with which they label those concepts. A decade ago a study in Yugoslavia *(23)* clearly revealed that newly enrolled first graders in Zagreb had much knowledge about nature, community institutions, local government, work, and personnel hygiene. The author concluded that most of this knowledge had been inculcated by families, because 88 percent of the children had never attended any preschool classes.

Children learn basic language patterns from their families and, in a landmark California study, Loban *(24)* concluded (as educators long had believed) that children who were deficient in oral language development almost invariably were retarded in reading development. This explains some of the findings in a number of other studies about the relationships between reading achievement and certain factors in the home environment.

Ketcham (21) used a questionnaire technique to study the backgrounds of 528 tenth grade students and as a result identified 26 family factors related to reading success at the .05 level of significance. The most important were: 1) the mother's use of the library; 2) the number of newspapers and good quality magazines in the home; and 3) the father's employment in professional, managerial, or technical work. Other factors of special value were visits to museums and places of historical interest, discussions by parents of news and other items read, giving of books as gifts, and hearing classical music in the home.

Goodson (17) gathered information through taped interviews about 21 pairs of good and poor readers who were matched on IQ. Good readers spent more time on hobbies, watching TV, listening to their radios, and playing their stereos. Their homes contained more books, magazines, and newspapers, and their parents attended more school functions than those of poor readers.

In Washington, D.C., in a study of 100 sixth grade pupils, Barra (2) found that there were significant correlations between reading achievement and attitudes of mothers toward education, aspirations for their children, and the levels of their own education.

In studying the environments of 20 eighth grade honor students, Napoli (31) observed that the usual family factors were related to reading achievement but, contrary to findings in most similar studies, the number of books in the home was not always important. Here the key word seems to be "always." Few things are always true.

Several of the studies already mentioned also identified home factors related to poor reading. In one study (17) it was noted that poor high school readers from low income homes spend more time on physical activities, including odd jobs, than do good readers. Also, poor readers have been found to be from less organized homes (2).

Ketcham (21) concluded low reading achievement was related to the negative views that: 1) only eggheads like to read, 2) reading is a feminine occupation, 3) college is only for those who can readily afford it, and 4) girls do not need a college education.

Not only is there a tendency for parents of poor readers to have less education (18), but parents who themselves were reading disabled often have children who are reading disabled (12).

Social-Emotional Comfort in Families

Concept development experiences supplied in the home provide an essential foundation for learning to read, but it appears that the emotional environment provided by the family may be equally important.

Maloney (26) found in a doctoral study at Fordham University that the preceptions of eighth grade girls concerning how their parents accepted them and used psychological controls on them were not significantly related to reading achievement. But Serwer (41), using transcriptions of group therapy sessions with college students who were attending a voluntary noncredit reading and study skills course at City College of New York, found that the students expressed feelings of hostility about faulty parent-child relationships which had persisted into early adult years. Some of these students traced the origin of their school problems to these interfamilial difficulties. In this respect, Peck (33) says that empirical and clinical-experimental studies, although limited, support the view that reading disorders indicate that relationships within the family are upset.

Stackhouse (44) compared interaction patterns within fifteen reading-problem families and fifteen normal families by using taped data and the Family Interaction Scales by Riskin and Faunce. He concluded that in the normal families there was more explicit agreement and explicit disagreement on various matters; families did not hide their opinions. The normal families also had more commitment to issues, ideas, suggestions, and to other family members. They tended to stay on a topic of discussion until they felt it was resolved, but would change topics to facilitate the progress of a discussion. These behaviors suggested that the family members were comfortable with each other and felt their opinions would be valued by others.

Gilmore (15) explains the need for emotional security for efficient learning by describing the importance of two mental activities—concentration and memory—in the learning process. He indicates that both of these mental activities are inhibited by social-emotional insecurity.

Gilmore has discovered that emotional conflict not only blocks concentration, but also defeats memory. And in the "utilization of memory lies one of the most pronounced differences between the underachiever and the higher achiever." Gilmore also notes that underachievers suffer from weak ego strength, while high achievers have strong egos, positive self-images, feelings of personal worth, and high degrees of motivation. He indicates that the sources of personality differences between high and low achievers "lie largely in the early home and family environments." More specifically:

> The high achiever's home has been found to be characterized by a strong, warm, and emphathic relationship between parents and children, as well as by good communication among family members ... mothers of high achievers gave them good verbal stimulation in early childhood, praised them for small accomplishments, and were attentive in responding to their question and requests for help . . . ."

Fortunately, children who come from troubled homes are not necessarily doomed to failure forever, because skillful educators may counsel parents and help to improve the situation. After four years' of research, Gilmore concludes that "a change in parents' fundamental attitudes toward children will transform underachieving students into highly motivated, productive ones" (15).

Frequent family moves generally are disruptive of family communications and individual social-emotional security. Therefore it is not surprising that, in studying 475 poor sixth grade readers in urban New York, Prior (35) found that school mobility was negatively related to achievement.

School and Family Teamwork

The research previously quoted suggests that families and schools should cooperate to provide more situations conducive to learning in the home. Studies indicate that families and schools can work together both in general child development and in programs where family members are trained to provide specific lessons related to reading and language development.

General Child Develpment

Artley (1) studied the backgrounds of successful reading teachers and found not only that good teachers promote the reading interests of their pupils but that the teachers' own family members had had a major influence on the development of *their* reading interests as children. Their parents had read to them and had made books and magazines readily available.

Macklin (25) compared the behaviors of nineteen young children who listened as adults read to them with behaviors of children who were not read to. The experimental children at age two were read to by fourteen year old working-class girls for twenty minutes daily, four days a week, for eight months. Then, for nine more months, the children were read to by their mothers or they participated in Head Start activities. Periodic measurements revealed that the experimental children consistently grew more in language than the control children, but that receptive language was the only specific facet where the differences was statistically significant. Although the parents and the teen readers were enthusiastic about the program, Macklin concluded that this procedure *alone* was not an adequate means for increasing the verbal facilities of children from low income families.

Families Trained to Promote Communication Skills

Because there is so much evidence to show that families have a profound impact upon children's capabilities in learning language and reading, a number of experiments have been undertaken to train parents in how to influence communications growth more significantly. Although the experiments have not always been as successful as was hoped, most have produced positive results.

One researcher (34) involved parents in directing three year old children to watch a television program entitled "Wordland Workshop" five days a week for thirty-nine weeks, while a control group watched "Captain Kangaroo." Parents gave experimental children assistance in learning the vocabulary skills introduced on TV. Posttest data and questionnaire findings revealed that the experimental group scored significantly higher on reading related skills than did the control group. Childrens' achievements in reading were positively correlated with parental competence and parental interest in the program.

Clegg (8) trained parents in the use of educational games to increase reading achievement of thirty second grade children from low income homes in Seattle. She found that after completing experimental games with their parents, the children in the experimental group had made significantly greater gains in reading vocabulary than the control group, but that their reading comprehension growth was not significantly greater. One possible explanation for this difference in skill growth is that most reading games focus on vocabulary more than on comprehension.

In addition to investigating the values of parental teaching programs, researchers also have attempted to determine whether home teaching programs are more effective when parents have special training than when they do not.

Crosset (11) involved parents of low income black children in Cincinnati for one school year in observing the children's reading instruction at school and then in supplementing it with planned instruction at home using materials obtained from a Famiy Learning Center located in the neighborhood. Reading achievement of children from families where parents participated in the training program was higher than that of children from nonparticipating families, but not to a significant degree. The program revealed the willingness of many parents to be involved, but possibly the quality of instruction depended too much on individual parent initiative in obtaining and using materials.

McKinney (28) taught parents of children from mixed ethnic backgrounds to tutor their children in reading and mathematics. They received two hours of training weekly for fifteen weeks. Later testing of pupils revealed that children of parents who had tutorial training achieved at a significantly higher level and had a significantly better attitude toward school than children from a control group of parents who had not learned the tutoring skills.

A team of researchers in Mesa, Arizona (46) trained a group of forty randomly selected kindergarten parents to teach specific reading readiness skills at home. The experimental parents received instruction twice a week in making reading games and in other readiness materials. The results of pre- and posttesting on the Murphy-Durrell Reading Readiness Test showed that the children of untrained parents learned to recognize the alphabet letters by name as well as children of trained parents. On the more difficult task of learning phonemes (letter sounds), however, the children of trained parents learned significantly more.

Sullivan and LaBeaune (45) attempted to prevent the usual summer decrement in academic achievement of kindergarten children by providing parents with directions for structured practice in reading related skills. Not only did they prevent the decrement, but they found that parent instruction resulted in the children's postsummer achievement being higher than it was at the beginning of the summer.

Recently the Home and School Institute at Trinity College in Washington, D.C., offered a fascinating book called *A Family Affair: Education*. It contains clever "home learning recipes" that parents can use to capture their youngsters' interests with simple educational activities that make "home the learning place." One experiment revealed that first grade children who used these recipes achieved significantly higher reading scores than children in control classes (39).

Because of the need for constructive relationships in family learning situations, Goldman (16) conducted a field study at the University of Pittsburgh to determine whether six mothers of underachieving low income children could be trained to be involved in their children's learning and whether they could increase the number of positively reinforcing behaviors they used with youngsters. All of the mothers participated readily and learned several techniques for informal teaching. Most reduced the negative comments they made to their children and greatly increased the number of informal positive reinforcers they used to encourage learning.

Children Tutoring Children

In Jamaica, Robinson (*38*) found that volunteer tutors were more understanding of and more effective in teaching adult illiterates than teachers. Similarly, a research team in the United States (*20*) proved that high school students could tutor young elementary children as effectively as parents could. Numerous additional studies have shown that children of different ages can successfully teach certain skills to those of younger ages. Eberwein and others (*13*) reviewed thirty-four studies of tutoring, and Bloom (*3*) condensed the findings from several others in a small book entitled *Peer and Cross-Age Tutoring in the Schools.* Bloom says that "the consensus appears to be that a wide range of ages, experiences, levels of achievement, cultural backgrounds, and intelligence levels may characterize successful tutors."

In sampling the studies one finds that children in experimental tutored groups made significantly greater gains than those in untutored groups when sixth graders tutored third graders (*4*); when seventh and eighth graders tutored children in grades one through four (*5*); when tenth and eleventh graders tutored elementary pupils (*9*); and when eighth graders tutored fourth, fifth, and sixth graders (*42*). Mexican-American pupils succeeded in tutoring younger children (*29*) just as pupils representing other ethnic groups did. Although peer and cross-age tutoring programs have not been equally successful under all circumstances, it seems almost certain that most schools can make them succeed.

Obviously, children should be able to learn from their own siblings at least as well as they do from the pupil tutors in schools. In reviewing a collection of studies on siblings teaching siblings, Cicirelli (*7:100-101*) noted that sibling tutors have several advantages over nonsibling tutors:

> There is greater opportunity for family peers to provide reinforcement and modeling for each other. The closeness of the family leads to greater empathy, rapport, and communications. In the family, the child is better able to view things from his peer's viewpoint, speak the same language, and understand his problems and learning difficulties. Most important is the long-range advantage of siblings teaching siblings. If siblings teach each other, they will develop caring relationships and will turn to each other for help . . . .

Research to date suggests that "if the older sibling is a girl or widely spaced in age from the younger sibling, effects are more positive than if the older sibling is a boy or close in age" (Cicirelli, 1976, p. 108). It has been observed that girls and older boys are more likely than younger boys to give many examples and explanations in teaching their siblings. An interesting related finding is that boys who are given responsibility for caring for younger siblings at home, tend to become more attentive themselves in the school learning situation (14).

Even without such empirical evidence, teachers know that siblings teach siblings. Frequently when children are already reading upon entering school, the teacher will discover they learned to read when they played school at home with other children.

All of these findings on tutoring by nonsiblings and by siblings provide undeniable evidence that children in the home can be a major resource for helping their siblings learn language and reading skills. But currently children in large families tend to read more poorly than those in small families (37). Obviously, schools and parents need to give careful consideration to ways in which older children in a family can be pleasantly and systematically involved in educational activities to benefit younger children.

Summary and Recommendations

The research that has been reviewed here can be summarized in a few generalizations:

1. Many children probably gain a somewhat greater amount of functional knowledge from the home and the community than they do from the school.
2. Good readers come from home environments that are psychologically comfortable, that foster positive attitudes toward reading and learning, and that provide stimulating cultural and language experiences.
3. Parents who are encouraged or are trained to do so can be effective in providing cultural experiences and many simple learning experiences.
4. Siblings, as well as aunts, uncles, and grandparents, can make valuable contributions through informal tutoring.

Because of the importance of winning the support of families in the reading development of their children, the IRA Commission on Teacher Development has recommended that the professional education of every teacher should include a module on Interaction with Parents and the Community (40). The module written by Nichols (32) is an example of those that have been developed in detail and used in teacher education programs. Also, a vast number of publications of other types are available for use by teachers to involve parents in educational support activities.

The advancement of the health, happiness, productiveness, and ethical standards of humankind are very much dependent upon high levels of literacy. But the financially pressed schools of the world have difficulty performing at expected levels. Educators must, therefore, place a high priority upon developing and utilizing family resources.

Bibliography and References

1. ARTLEY, A. STERL. "Successful Teachers of Reading: Who Are They?" paper presented at the International Reading Association's annual convention, Denver, May 1973. (Eric Document ED 074454)
2. BARRA, JULIA A. "Selected Cultural Variables and the Reading Achievement of Black Innercity School Children of Washington, D.C.," doctoral dissertation, Catholic University of America, 1973. Dissertation Abstracts International, 34 (3-A) (1973), 1057. (Eric Document P 550203102)
3. BLOOM, SOPHIE. Peer and Cross-Age Tutoring in the Schools. Washington, D.C.: U.S. Department of Health, Education, and Welfare, 1976.
4. BOYD, G. S. "Reading Achievement and Personal Adjustment: A Study of the Effects of Participation as a Tutor and as a Pupil in an Elementary School Tutorial Reading Program," doctoral dissertation, University of Alabama at Tuscaloosa, 1969.
5. BREMMER, BARBARA L. Students Helping Students Program, 1971-1972, final report. Washington, D.C.: U.S. Office of Education, 1972. (Eric Document ED 074473)
6. CHOMSKY, CAROL. "Stages in Language Development and Reading Exposure," Harvard Educational Review, 42, 1 (1972), 1-33. (Eric Document EJ 055650)
7. CICIRELLI, VICTOR G. "Siblings Teaching Siblings," in Vernon L. Allen (Ed.), Children as Teachers. New York: Academic Press, 1976.
8. CLEGG, BLANCHE. "The Effectiveness of Learning Games Used By Economically Disadvantaged Parents to Increase the Reading Achievement of Their Children," paper presented at the annual meeting of American Educational Research Association, New Orleans, March 1973. (Eric Document ED 085656)
9. CLOWARD, R. D. "Studies in Tutoring," Journal of Experimental Education, 36 (1967), 14-25.

10. COONS, JOHN E., and STEPHEN D. SUGARMAN. *Education by Choice: The Case for Family Control.* Berkeley: University of California Press, 1978.

11. CROSSET, ROBERT J., JR. "The Extent and Effect of Parents' Participation in Their Children's Beginning Reading Program: An Innercity Project," doctoral dissertation, University of Cincinnati, 1972. University Microfilms, No. 72-31, 922. (Eric Document ED 076946)

12. DELKER, DARYL L. *The Role of Heredity in Reading Disability.* Glassboro, New Jersey: Glassboro State College, 1971. (Eric Document ED 050923)

13. EBERWEIN, LOWELL, and others. "An Annotated Bibliography on Volunteer Tutoring Programs," paper presented at the Southeast Regional Reading Conference of IRA, 1976. (Eric Document ED 117662)

14. GALLIMORE, RONALD, ROLAND G. THARP, and GISELA E. SPEIDEL. "The Relationship of Sibling Caretaking and Attentiveness to a Peer Tutor," *American Educational Research Journal*, 15 (1978), 267-273.

15. GILMORE, JOHN V. "Parental Influence on Academic Achievement," *Normline*, 2, 2. New York: Harcourt Brace Jovanovich, undated.

16. GOLDMAN, RICHARD. "Development of a Training Program to Increase the Use of Reinforcers in Informal Teaching by Mothers of Educationally Disadvantaged Children," doctoral dissertation, University of Pittsburgh, 1970.

17. GOODSON, FLOYD L. "Factors Related to Success in Reading by Disadvantaged Children," doctoral dissertation, University of Arizona, 1974. *Dissertation Abstracts International*, 34 (8-A) (1974), 4559. (Eric Document P 550408156)

18. HECKERL, JOHN R., and RUSSELL J. SANSBURY. "A Study of Severe Reading Retardation," *Reading Teacher*, 21, 8 (1968), 724-729. (Eric Document P 420017795)

19. HENDERSON, ANDREW G. "Training in Attention Development As Related to Cognitive Style and Reading Performance among Disadvantaged Children," doctoral dissertation, Hofstra University, 1974. *Dissertation Abstracts International*, 34 (10-B) (1974), 5222. (Eric Document P 550613164)

20. KEELE, REBA L., and GRANT V. HARRISON. "The Effects of Parents Using Structured Tutoring Techniques in Teaching Their Children to Read," paper presented at meeting of AERA, New York, 1971. (Eric Document ED 047926)

21. KETCHAM, CLAY A. "The Home Background and Reader Self-Concept which Relate to Reading Achievement," doctoral dissertation, Lehigh University, 1966. *Dissertation Abstracts*, 28 (2-A) (1967), 499. (Eric Document P 420004485)

22. KREUL, WILLIAM R. "An Analysis of the Effects of a Preschool Program for Parental Involvement on Reading Readiness," doctoral dissertation, University of North Dakota, 1975. University Microfilms No. 76-5002. (Eric Document ED 119165)

23. KUSTREBA, T. Ispitivanje predznanja djece prilikom upisa u prvi razred osnovne skole ("Testing the Level of Knowledge of Children of Enrollment in the First Grade of Primary School"), *Pedagogska Iskustva*, Zagreb, 1 (1968), 4-48. (Eric Document ED 060350)

24. LOBAN, WALTER D. *The Language of Elementary School Children.* Urbana, Illinois: National Council of Teachers of English, 1963.

25. MACKLIN, ELEANOR D. "Evaluation of a Program Designed to Affect the Language Development of Young Disadvantaged Children," doctoral dissertation, Cornell University, 1974. *Dissertation Abstracts International*, 34 (12-A) (1974), 7589. (Eric Document P 550613195)

26. MALONEY, PATRICIA M. "Perceived Parental Child Rearing Patterns, Field Articulation, and Reading Achievement in Eighth Grade Girls," doctoral dissertation, Fordham University, 1974. *Dissertation Abstracts International*, 35 (3-A), (1974), 1503. (Eric Document P 550613321)

27. McDONALD, FREDERICK M. "Report on Phase II of the Beginning Teacher Evaluation Study," *Journal of Teacher Education*, 27 (1976), 39-42.

28. McKINNEY, JOHN A. "The Development and Implementation of a Tutorial Program for Parents to Improve the Reading and Mathematics Achievement of Their Children," doctoral dissertation, Nova University, 1975. (Eric Document ED 113703)

29. MORITA, H. "The Effects of Cross-Age Tutoring on the Reading Achievement and Behavior of Selected Elementary Grade Children," doctoral dissertation, University of Southern California at Los Angeles, 1972.

30. MUSTAPHA, NIK FAIZAH. "Case Study: Malaysia," in George Sullivan, *A Reason to Read: A Report on an International Symposium on the Promotion of the Reading Habit*. New York: Academy for Educational Development and Unesco, 1976, 47-49.

31. NAPOLI, JOSEPH. "Environmental Factors and Reading Ability," *Reading Teacher*, 21, 6 (1968), 552-557, 607. (Eric Document P 420017806)

32. NICHOLS, EDITH. *Interaction with Parents and the Community: An Instructional Module*. Warrensburg, Missouri: Central Missouri State University, 1975 (mimeographed).

33. PECK, BRUCE B. "Reading Disorders: Have We Overlooked Something?" *Journal of School Psychology*, 9, 2 (1971), 182-190. (Eric Document EJ 045082)

34 PERLISH, HARVEY N. *Wordland Workshop*. Philadelphia: Radio and Television Division, Triangle Publications, 1968. (Eric Document ED 025946)

35. PRIOR, DANIEL R. "Innercity Elementary Pupil Mobility, Reading Achievement, and Environmental Process Variables," doctoral dissertation, Fordham University, 1974. *Dissertation Abstracts International*, 35 (3-A), (1974), 1509-1510. (Eric Document P 550613333)

36. RAHIMI, NASSAR. "Case Study: Iran," in George Sullivan, *A Reason to Read: A Report on an International Symposium on the Promotion of the Reading Habit*. New York: Academy for Educational Development and Unesco, 1976, 41-44.

37. RICHARDSON, K. "Reading Attainment and Family Size: An Anomaly," *British Journal of Educational Psychology*, 47 (February 1977), 71-75.

38. ROBINSON, JOYCE L. "Case Study: Jamaica," in George Sullivan, *A Reason to Read: A Report on an International Symposium on the Promotion of the Reading Habit*. New York: Academy for Educational Development and Unesco, 1976, 44-47.

39. SANDERS, TONYA. "Home's Simplest Items Can Help a Child Learn," *Washington Star*, December 7, 1977.

40. SARTAIN, HARRY W., and PAUL STANTON (Eds.). *Modular Preparation for Teaching Reading*. Newark, Delaware: International Reading Association, 1974.

41. SERWER, BLANCHE L. "The Relation between Parent-Child Interaction and Inadequacy in College Reading and Study," paper presented at annual congress of Inner-American Society of Psychology, Mexico City, December 1967. (Eric Document ED 016589)

42. SHERERTZ, D. *Ontario-Montclair School District Evaluation Summary: Cross-Age Teaching*. Ontario, California, 1970.

43. SMITH, CARL B. *Parents and Reading.* Newark, Delaware: Internatonal Reading Association, 1971.
44. STACKHOUSE, THOMAS W. "A Communication Analysis of the Art of Being Stupid: A Family Systems and Communication Approach to the Study of Families with Children Having Reading Problems," doctoral dissertation, University of Georgia, 1974. *Dissertation Abstracts International,* 34 (7-A) (1974), 3890. (Eric Document P 550407406)
45. SULLIVAN, HOWARD J., and CAROL LaBEAUNE. "Effects of Parent-Administered Summer Reading Instruction," paper presented at the AERA meeting, Minneapolis, March 1970. (Eric Document ED 042831)
46. WOODS, CAROL, and others. *The Effect of the Parent Involvement Program on Reading Readiness Scores.* Mesa, Arizona: Mesa Public Schools, 1974. (Eric Document ED 104527)

Additional References and Resources

BREILING, ANNETTE. "Using Parents as Teaching Partners," *Reading Teacher,* 30 (1976), 187-192.

CHAN, JULIE M. T. *Why Read Aloud to Children?* Newark, Delaware: International Reading Association, 1974. (Eric Document ED 097649)

DEGENARO, JENNIE J. "What Do You Say When a Parent Asks, How Can I Help My Child?" *Journal of Learning Disabilities,* 6, 2 (1973), 102-105. (Eric Document EJ 074668)

ELDER, RACHEL ANN, et al. *Minicourse in Tutoring in Reading.* San Francisco, California: Far West Laboratory for Educational Research and Development, 1973.

FRESHOUR, FRANK W. "Beginning Reading: Parents Can Help," *Reading Teacher,* 25, 6 (1972), 513-516.

GARCIA, RICARDO L., and RITA M. DEYOE. *Cómo ayudar a su niño a aprender a leer Inglés como segunda lengua* (Spanish translation of *How Can I Help My Child Learn to Read English As a Second Language?* by Marcia Baghban). Newark, Delaware: International Reading Association, 1972. (Eric Document ED 112361)

GORDON, IRA J., and WILLIAM F. BREVIOGEL. *Building Effective Home-School Relationships.* Boston: Allyn and Bacon, 1977.

GROTBERG, EDITH H. "Parent Roles in Fostering Reading," in Michael Labuda (Ed.), *Creative Reading for Gifted Learners: A Design for Excellence.* Newark, Delaware: International Reading Association, 1974, 34-45.

HICKS, JANET. "Parents' Day," *Early Years,* 8 (October 1977), 53-54.

HOSKISSON, KENNETH. "Should Parents Teach Their Children to Read?" *Elementary English,* 51, 2 (1974), 295-299. (Eric Document EJ 092562)

KOPPMAN, PATRICIA S. "Taking Reading Home," *Reporting on Reading* (Cemrel), June 1978, 1-2, 8.

MILLER, JULANO. *Helping Your LD Child at Home.* San Rafael, California: Academic Therapy Publications, 1973.

O'BRIAN, KATHY. "Household Aides," *Early Years,* October 1977, 52-53.

PETERSON, KAREN S. "Parent Intervention Effect on Achievement, Self-Concept, and Internal and Home Responsibilities in Elementary School Students," *Dissertation Abstracts International,* 36, 8 (1975), 50-55.

PICKERING, C. THOMAS. *Helping Children Learn to Read: A Primer for Adults.* New York: Chesford, 1977.

QUATTROCKI, CAROLYN (Ed.). *Creative Family Fun*. Athens, Ohio: Teacher Corps Program, College of Education, Ohio University, 1977.

RICH, DOROTHY, and CYNTHIA JONES. *A Family Affair: Education*. Washington, D.C.: Home School Institute, Trinity College, 1977.

RICH, DOROTHY, and CYNTHIA JONES. *The Three Rs Plus*. Washington, D.C.: Home School Institute, Trinity College, 1978.

RIZZO, THERESA E. "Home Parental Assistance for Underachieving Readers in Third Grade Using Read-at-Home Program Kits," *Dissertation Abstracts International*, 37 (6-A) (1976), 3473.

ROBERSON, DOROTHY R. "Parents and Teachers: Partners in the Teaching of Reading," *Reading Teacher*, 23 (1970), 722-726.

ROGERS, NORMA. *How Can I Help My Child Get Ready to Read?* Newark, Delaware: International Reading Association, 1972.

SOVIERO, MARGARET C. *Reading Recognition Readiness* (activity charts). Early-Childhood Education Development, Box 145, McMurray, Pennsylvania 15317.

STAHL, NORMAN A. "22 Ways to Harness Parent Power," *Early Years*, 8 (October 1977), 56.

SULLIVAN, HOWARD J., and CAROL LaBRAUNE. "Parents: Summer Reading Teachers," *Elementary School Journal*, 5 (1971), 279-285.

TREGASKIS, GEORGE K., and others. *Learning Experiences at Home: Reinforcement for the Early School Program*. Albany, New York: New York State Education Department, 1974. (Eric Document ED 105995)

WOLF, ALINE D. *Tutoring Is Caring: You Can Help Someone to Read*. Tutoring Works, 2733 Sixth Avenue, Altoona, Pennsylvania.

YERKOVICH, RAY. "Project Earlychild," *Early Years*, 8 (October 1977), 55, 58.

Your Child and Reading: How You Can Help. Boston: Houghton Mifflin, 1973.

Opportunities to Use Family Resources for Reading in the Developing Countries of Africa

Martha I. B. McSwain
Alvan Ikoku College of Education
Owerri, Imo State
Nigeria

It is with a great deal of pleasure that I share some of my thoughts on how reading can be promoted by the African family. I have lived for nearly three years in Eastern Nigeria and do not pretend to be knowlegeable about life elsewhere on the vast continent of Africa. My research and personal contacts, however, support the generalizations I have made.

"The family is by far the most important primary group in society. In fact, of all human organizations none transcends the family in the intensity of sociological significance" (*21*). An Igbo, himself, the writer makes this observation of his own Eastern Nigerian group. Casual observers and scholars alike agree unequivocally that the family is the strongest, most cohesive, and most viable societal unit in the African context. Family influence is, therefore, felt in every human endeavor, whether political, educational, religious, or economic. That its impact upon literacy and reading be given serious examination is both judicious and expedient.

Reading as Literacy

It is the opinion of this writer that "literacy" and "reading" do not and should not convey the same meaning. Literacy equips individuals with certain skills which enable them to derive meaning from any printed materials they encounter in their day-to-day activities. Reading is an all-encompassing concept for it embodies not only the possession of literacy skills but also their constant use for the purpose of acquiring information and for enjoyment. Literacy is a skeleton upon which the robust flesh of reading rests. Today in the developing countries of Africa, reading is considered one of the three literacy skills; the second is writing; and the third, numeracy. For most Africans reading is meant to be functional, a means to the practical end of earning money and moving up the socioeconomic ladder. Probably this attitude is directly related to the level of development; education must aim at producing something or helping the particular country to rise quickly to prominence in the family of nations. Most African nations cannot yet afford the luxury of education for education's sake. Therefore, this paper does not focus on the idea of enriched reading, but on "literacy" as functional "reading."

The Concept of "Family" in Africa
The Extended Family

"The fact is that most Africans take a broader view of family relationship and responsibility than do most Westerners" (Moore and Dunbar, 1968). The *etuka* or extended family of the Ngombe of the northwestern part of the Republic of the Congo may consist of two, three, or four segments, each composed of three to eight adult males with their children and their sisters. Or it may include only the families of siblings (male and female), or the families of the sons of siblings, the patrilocal organization (Bascom and Henskovits, 1959).

The polygamous family of the polygenous type is a structure which includes a man and two or more wives and their children. It is also predominantly partrilineal and patrilocal, with males enjoying authority as well as inheritance. Pockets of matrilineal groups are found in various locations on the continent but are weakening and being overtaken by the worldwide phenomenon of male domination. The Sagara of Tanzania, the Congo of Zaire, the Ashanti of Ghana, the Bemba of Zambia, the Chewa of Malawi, and the Ohaffia of Nigeria are examples of matrilineal systems which are still in existence (Shorter 1973, p. 165).

Another family structure may consist of several households in which live the head of the family, his wife or wives, and their unmarried children. The husbands and children of married daughters may constitute an integral part of matri-local families such as occur among the Ohaffia, the only matrilineal and matrilocal Nigerian people (Nsugbe 1974). Among matrilineal groups the husband joins the family of the wife. Inheritance, as well, passes through the female members.

An extended family may embrace relatives, both close and distant, gathered under the guardianship of one male who, by virtue of his economic circumstances, has accepted full responsibility for their welfare, upbringing, and training. His own wife or wives and children are completely integrated into the larger family community. It is often not possible for an observer to distinguish between the biological offspring of the "master" and the other relatives.

The monogamous nuclear family of the Western type is gaining acceptance in some African societies, especially where Christianity has triumphed over earlier tradition and where increased educational opportunities are making every new generation less and less dependent upon the previous one.

Ever present in most African households are those individuals whose presence is meant solely for the purpose of rendering service to members of the family circle. These "servants" may, indeed, be some of the relatives who exchange their services for the protecton and training accorded them by the head of the family—the young children of a deceased elderly father whose last young wife recently bore them or perhaps the children of a former age-mate who has met with misfortune. Regardless of their individual responsibilities, all may be called upon (as they frequently are) to minister to the needs of the head of the household. Whether the master (or mistress, as the case may be) is African or non-African, servants tend to identify with the family they serve and the master reciprocates. Servants may grow up, marry, and begin their own families while still in the service of the one master.

It is not uncommon for the master to become involved with the education of the children of his servants. This involvement may include payment of the school fees or could simply mean intervention with school authorities on behalf of the children. In a sense, the master accepts the children of his servants as his personal responsibility.

Age Groups

Age grades, age sets, and generation sets constitute other important societal groups which differ from the extended family. Membership is associated with chronological age, the age of circumcision, or descent and kinship. The ties that bind these individual groups together are, in certain respects, more capable of surviving perilous dividing influences than familial ties. Quoting Kenyatta, one writer says of one Kikuyu subset, "Men circumcised at the same time stand in the very closest relationship to each other. When a man of the same age group injures another, it is a serious magicoreligious offense. They are like blood brothers; they must not do any wrong to each other. It ranks with an injury done to a member of one's own family" (Middleton and Kershaw, 1972, p. 36). The group may function as a social, economic, or political institution and may for a defined purpose join other age groups until the mission or task is accomplished. More will be said about the nature of some of the activities of the age groups. For the moment, suffice it to say that, depending upon their constituency and leadership, they are capable of being powerful agents for change and for improving educational opportunities.

Ethnic Groups

Ethnocentrism is a quality that generally conveys a pejorative idea. Yet it is a quality that is so much a facet of the African character that most Africans will work untiringly to accomplish anything that will make their own ethnic group appear to be superior to another. Good as well as evil forces can take advantage of this human quality.

Other Social Groups

Religious groups (especially those patterned after modern secular establishments), social and political community organizations, and professional and trade unions are making their collective influence felt in many quarters. On certain sensitive issues, they may speak out with the fervor of a family whose very survival is at stake, so closely do they identify with each other. In *African Culture and the Christian Church* Shorter says that in Africa, "what matters are the social relationships on which they are based" (Shorter, 1973, p. 157).

Clearly then, in Africa, "family" is an idea rather than a fixed entity, but the family unit is cohesive and exerts strong influence on its members. "It would be unrealistic and quite presumptuous to predict the dissolution of the family community . . ." (Shorter, 1974, p. 71). Personal observation leads one to conclude that there is little reason to believe that the Western concept of "family" will overshadow or uproot the African family tradition in the near future, if ever.

Family Resources

Children

On a continent where offsprings are considered a married couple's most cherished possessions, children must be considered an extremely valuable family resource. Most African women begin producing children as soon as they are married and may continue doing so throughout their productive years. People in all classes prize the large family for its social and educative value. The implications for a polygamous family are obvious. This writer was personally acquainted with a chief who, at the time of his death, had three wives and twenty-three children. Even though large families are the rule rather than the exception, few parents, even chiefs, have the means with which to educate all of their children. Hence, some are chosen to go to school while the others remain at home to wait for the later assistance of the more fortunate ones. In many cases, help is sought from outsiders or other family members.

Males

Male children are regarded as special assets to most families, their importance being exemplified in a number of practices. In Nigerian Igbo culture, a woman who during her productive years fails to produce a male child can prevent one of her daughters (usually the eldest) from marrying until she produces one or more male children for her parents. As soon as a Kikuyu (Kenya) child is born, the mother emits five screams if it is a boy and four if it is a girl (Middleton and Kershaw, 1972, p. 54). Most African societies are patrilineal and patrilocal. Females have no rights of inheritance. In fact, in some cultures married females are no longer considered a part of their parents' family, but become a part of their husband's family. In many African societies only males are permitted to go to school. In Benin (formerly Dahomey) "More boys than girls are educated, and in some families one boy in two is educated" (Skinner, 1974, p. 197). One observer also noted that poor Moslems among the Yoruba in Nigeria still have doubts about sending girls to school (Southwest Jahoda, 1966, p. 170). This doubt is supported by many females and many more males. A young woman who is a personal acquaintance of the writer is an example. Although she is not literate, her literate husband is paying school fees for his two sisters. As the wife observed the two girls, she commented that her sisters-in-law were being "corrupted" by the other girls. Similarly, one young Nigerian male student wrote as a topic of his own choice that girls shouldn't receive education equal to that of boys because they will be troublesome and will begin to think they are equal to their husbands.

In the developing countries of Africa, various indexes show the literacy level to be from as low as 18 percent to as high as 50 percent. The great majority of the illiterate population is female, but the African male adults and the educated children constitute a major resource for improving education that cannot be overlooked.

Females

Among the few matrilineal groups, female authority must be reckoned with. When in conversation with a member of one of these groups, one is never left in doubt about the high regard in which females are held. One researcher writes, "These people are open about their strong bias toward their mothers and mothers' own kin group" (Nsugbe, 1974, p. 93).

Once a male student whispered to the writer, almost reverently, "We think so much of our women and girls" (Ude comment). Later it was noted that he was an Ohaffia. Apparently in some families women, as well as men, are resources to promote reading.

Elders

Elders are held in high esteem in African societies. In fact, most decisions about serious matters affecting the larger community are made by them with little or no opposition from younger members. Grandparents play an important role in the lives of children who spend a large part of their early years with them. Through this association children learn the folklore, the religious beliefs, and the social values and practices of the group.

Money

The resource that is in short supply for many African families is money. Although the majority of Africans are poor by Western standards, parents are prepared to spend as much on their children's education as their financial means permit, because they see education as the main channel for social and economic mobility. Since education is held in high regard, families will make a great effort to provide the funds or to obtain government aid for educating their children.

In developing Africa, the rate of illiteracy is high, most families are large and relatively poor, and neglect of the education of females is widespread. Positive influences for promoting literacy and reading are not readily discernable. But a closer look from the inside reveals that the African family's resources are unique and diversified, and if mobilized they have great potential for bringing reading to all.

Family Reading for Nutrition and Health: An Anecdote

Chioma ran home from school waving a leaf of paper in the air. It was a notice given to all of the children informing them of the visit to their school by some health officers who were coming the following day to administer the anti-measles vaccine to all preschool children. In every corner of Chioma's compound were small babies, some of whom were Chioma's sisters and brothers. "Go and visit the huts of your other mothers, Chioma. Read the notice to them very slowly and carefully so that they do not fail to take your sisters and brothers to have them protected." Chioma's mother was a teacher and she knew how important it was to have children inoculated against the diseases that had claimed the lives of far too many children in their village. Chioma's mother planned to visit them later to make it clear to her mates that their baby nurses should be given the same protection since many of them were not yet of school age. Besides, now that primary education was free they, too, would go to school in a few years.

The first child of her father, Chioma was happy to be the one who could read the newspapers to her other mothers as well as tell them how much medicine to give their babies and when to give it to them. Even though she was a girl, it was Chioma who had helped her village to produce more yams than any other in the entire division. Each day, after school, she had gone from compound to compound reading for the farmers of her extended family the directions on how to use the bags of free fertilizer the government had given them to implement a "Feed-the-Nation" program. She also went to the village church every Friday, the day their letters were delivered. While there, she helped many of her neighbors read their mail. It was a great honor for Chioma to be able to serve her elders. Chioma's father was working in a distant city. He had hoped that his first child would be a son, but now he was quite proud of his daughter who was doing so much to help his growing family. Her reading skill was a resource for many in the community, and the gratitude of her neighbors was motivation for her continued learning.

Family Resources for Language Learning

Since reading is the decoding of "talk written down," let us briefly examine the role of the family in the development of the most crucial of the prereading skills, language development.

Attitude toward the Language of Literacy

Children who receive their initial reading instruction in the language they have learned at home have a decided advantage over those who are faced with having to learn a second language for reading. In developing Africa, second language reading is probably "the greatest barrier to the development of good reading habits" (Kenyatta, 1962, p. 96). A carryover from the missionaries and the colonial days, literacy skills were taught so that the people "could absorb the lessons of the Bible" (Dike, 1976). On most of the continent, the languages of literacy are either English or French and not the local languages. On the whole, parents are so highly positive in their attitude toward literacy and education that Piaget's "extrinsic motivation for reading" (Furth, 1970, p. 4) is provided for second language learning as well. There are, however, a few scattered exceptions, as will be noted later.

Fathers

Fathers, who are usually better educated than the mothers, bring the language of literacy into the home. As the gulf in the social interrelationships between African fathers and their children narrows somewhat, greater opportunities are being afforded them to profit from the verbal exchange that heretofore did not take place. Fathers, brothers, and select educated members of the extended family now have a major role to play in bringing the language of literacy to the children at home. Since the commitment to universal primary education by all the African countries in attendance at the Unesco Conference at Addis Ababa in 1961 (Jahoda, undated, 168), family economic constraints have been relaxed, thus bringing children of all classes out of the compounds and into the schools. Many are attending free elementary schools, with the enrollment of girls showing a dramatic increase. Even in some male dominated societies one hears fathers making the statement that "To educate a daughter is to educate a family."

Other Adult Models

The ethnic group among whom I live are a highly verbal people. No matter the level of education, or the absence of it, a ready oration seems to be on the tip of every adult tongue. Opportunities for speech-making are not lacking in this culture, for the Igbos seize every opportunity for a social gathering during which many hours are spent in oratory.

A twelve year old Igbo girl who accompanied me to the United States attracted interviewers from a number of newspapers and radio and television stations. On two separate occasions she found herself standing before a microphone and an audience of more than one hundred people. She proved more than up to the tasks even though she was struggling with a language that was not her own. The influence of her adult models was clearly exemplified in her self-confidence and her ability to make herself understood in spite of her lack of fluency in English.

The same degree of verbal self-confidence is seen in children who participate in local radio and television programs, some of which are in the vernacular, others in the second language.

Children learn speech in the vernacular very early as they listen to the lullabies, stories, and lessons while snuggling close to the back of mother or nurse. "At the time when the child begins to learn how to speak, care is taken by the mother to teach him or her the correct manner of speech and to acquaint him with all important names in the family, past and present" (Nwagwu 1976, p. 9). When children are able to speak, they can answer questions which are asked gently and naturally. In short, they are learning language painlessly and effortlessly without knowing they are being taught by the mother language model. This infant tutoring by mothers is a major contribution to reading readiness in children.

Siblings

In order to relieve mothers of some of their child rearing responsibilities so that they can attend to other duties, sisters and brothers who are slightly older (but scarcely larger) carry their younger siblings about on their backs, amusing them with the conversation, stories, and songs which they, themselves, learned in the same way. Consequently these siblings are another major resource for prereading language development.

The Family Radio

In nearly every African home, no matter how modest, some member of the family has acquired a radio. Ranging from an elaborate stereo, two-speaker system, to a tiny one-battery set the family's radio is the primary source of music and entertainment from the "outside." In addition, many stations are using this medium to bring a variety of educational programs to the masses. Language for literacy is one of the priorities. Listening and learning songs in another language is another easy, almost natural, route to a second language. The family radio is an investment that will continue paying dividends by providing a model for second language learning.

Family Resources for Reading

Siblings

According to Nwagwu, "In Africa, thirty-four countries have free primary education, but it is not compulsory in most of these nations, and eighteen countries have neither free nor compulsory primary education" (Nwagwu, 1976, p.9). In these nations, economic constraints mandate selectivity within large families trying to educate their children. Those who are chosen are obligated to teach basic reading to those who must wait at home. The efforts of these select members can go a long way toward bringing limited functional literacy to adult members of the extended family. Child literacy can grow also from familiarity with family stories, as illustrated below.

Original Stories in the Absence of Books

Kawuba was now in class three. He had done well in school. Today, his English teacher had asked the class to write about something they would always remember, an unforgettable event. Should he write about one of the wonderful stories his old grandfather used to relate as all of the children of their compound gathered beneath the bright *harmatan* moon? A spell engulfed the compound as these wonderful tales of many generations unwound. Kawuba knew them so well. And there was one day in his life that Kawuba would never forget, even if he lived to be as old as his grandfather who lived to one hundred and one. This was his story.

THE RED TROUSERS for KAWUBA

The August break had given way to the early September rains. Kawuba lay on his bed listening to the "Kpom kpom kpom" of the rain on the zinc roof of his house. Sleep refused to come, even though darkness had descended upon the compound more than an hour ago.

The moon shared a white string that cut across Kawuba's pillow and a bit of the collar of his new school uniform which was tucked securely underneath. "I will keep this here," he said, after his mother had pressed his shirt and trousers. "When the time comes, I shall know where it is and be ready."

Turning over on his bed, Kawuba closed his eyes. But somehow, his eyes refused to cooperate. He found himself standing at his mother's bedroom door, tapping softly to say that it was time for him to have his morning bath. Kawuba did not really want his mother to give him his morning bath any more. After all, he was a big boy starting school. He could bathe himself.

"Why is it so dark?" thought Kawuba as he heard his mother say, "Go back to your bed, Kawuba. It is not yet time to get up!"

When sleep finally came, Kawuba found himself in the school compound, playing with children he did not know. "Go away!" shouted a boy who was taller than Kawuba. "This school is for big boys and girls, not for babies like you!"

Kawuba woke up with a start, greatly relieved to find that he had been dreaming. But why hadn't his mother come to call him to prepare for school? Could she have forgotten that today was to be his first day to go to school?

Carefully lifting one corner of his pillow, Kawuba checked his new uniform to be sure that the blue pants and white shirt were not becoming wrinkled. Suddenly the school pants were transformed into the beautiful red trousers his mother had promised him if he scored high marks in the first examination.

"Yes, mother has forgotten," though Kawuba. "I must go and wake her up." Although Kawuba had not heard the usual morning clatter of water pails, he was convinced that it was time to get up to get ready.

"Go back to your bed, Kawuba; it is not yet time to get up!" came his mother's voice from the other side of her bedroom door.

"Why is this night so much longer than all of the others?" thought Kawuba as he trudged dejectedly back to his room. He was sure he had heard the last cock crow hours ago.

Determined not to allow himself to be late, Kawuba decided to sit on his *oche* near the open window to wait for daybreak. With one more peek at his uniform, Kawuba settled himself on the wooden *oche* his father had made for him when he was a much smaller boy. He would need a new one soon, one more suitable for a big boy.

"Kukororo Okoo," crowed Kawuba's own rooster from the woodpile in back of the yam barn. Kawuba had dozed and had nearly fallen from his seat. He knew that his own rooster would not deceive him; it was time. Besides, Kawuba thought he could discern a faint

McSwain

glimmer of brightness in the sky beyond the ugbaka trees that lined the main road.

"Everybody must look clean and neat at school," explained Kawuba's mother as she rubbed his neck briskly with a fresh towel from the shelf.

"He looks fine," exclaimed Kawuba's father, who had delayed going to work this morning so that he could see his son depart for school on his first day. "Your mother says she promised you a new pair of red trousers, Kawuba. I have given her money to buy them if you score well in your examination"

With a downward glance, Kawuba answered softly, "I shall try my best, father." He collected his blue exercise book and the new white pencil his big sister had given him as a starting-school present.

Kawuba was happy with everything he saw in the school compound. He was also happy that there was no big boy to tease him. At times he went closer to the teacher so that he would not miss any part of her stories. His mother would be happy if he could repeat the stories to her when he went home.

When the examination was given, Kawuba listened intently to every instruction the teacher gave. He had learned the English alphabet with his sister's help. He even knew how to say many things in English, although he spoke and understood Igbo best. His sister had taught him how to count and his mother had often played counting games with him as he helped her sort the kola nuts which she sometimes sold. He also knew how to read and write his name.

When the marks were put up on the wall, Kawuba saw that his own name was the first on the list. There were some other words on the chart that Kawuba could not read, but he knew what "first" meant and he knew that he would be put in class "A". Most important of all, he knew that his mother would buy him the new red trousers.

The teacher called him to the front of the class and told the other children to clap for him.

Kawuba's embarrassment was exceeded only by the happiness he felt as he ran home to give his mother the good news.

When Kawuba returned home that day, his little sister Nwamaka who was in elementary four ran to him shouting as she always did, "What do you have for me, Kawuba?" He had printed his assignment on sheets of foolscap given to him by the teacher. Kawuba handed it to Nwamaka. Excitedly she sat down on her *oche* to try to read her brother's story. She ran to her mother who was plaiting six-year-old Chinyere's hair. "Would you like to hear Kawuba's story, mother?" Chinyere and her mother listened as Nwamaka proudly read her brother's words. "Oh, Kawuba," squealed Chinyere, "We like your story. Will you write another one for us?"

Modern African writers are indebted to their elders who through oral tradition, have provided the themes for many of their works. A true picture of African life is being projected to the world through the proliferation of novels, poetry, and prose throughout the continent. Even from obscure teacher institutions come delightful stories that, if put into print, would captivate children of any clime. "Red Trousers for Kawuba" is one of them.

Age Grades

The activities of age mates range from pooling their individual resources in order to send one of their members abroad to a university to laying a water pipeline in their home community. The building of schools and public buildings and the construction of roads and bridges are other examples of the self-help that has contributed immensely to development all over Africa. Age mates have played a major role in these projects. As their plans unfold in the future, attention must be given especially to the inclusion of libraries which are woefully underprovided at present.

Ethnic Groups

In some African countries certain inequities in educational attainment exist among the ethnic groups, inequities which are traceable to the acceptance by some, and the rejection by others, of the language of literacy. In Northern Nigeria, for example, the Hausas have, on religious grounds, traditionally been skeptical about the use of the English language for basic instruction in schools. A predominantly Moslem culture, this group sees the use of English, particularly in the early years, as an avenue that leads to the exposure of their children to the "corrupting influences" of Western education. They tend to teach children in Hausa for the first three years of school, delaying full-time formal English teaching until the fourth year. Arabic, the preferred language of the Koran, is studied by most elementary school boys in private classes after regular school hours. Since some boys learn a different tribal language at home before Hausa, they must have mastered four languages before they finish the seven year elementary school. Obviously this is a major burden when learning to read. At the World Confederation of Organizations of the Teaching Profession in August 1977, Northern Nigerian teachers expressed dismay at the level of achievement in reading among their students when compared to other sections of the country and they attributed it to the prevailing attitude toward the language of literacy. In nations that have no native *lingua franca*, but use a second language for the official language as well as for the predominant language of learning, ethnic and religious factions would be wise to rethink their stand on the language issue in order not to deny their children every opportunity of competing favourably with their counterparts in other sections of the country. While establishing a native lingua franca may be a desirable goal, "it is easier said than done" (Ukeje, 1977). A more realistic and less idealistic stand by those concerned could help to dispel the existing myth of the ethnic superiority of certain groups.

Buying Books

Books are valued treasures in Africa. A little boy in Ghana wanted to carry my bag for money "to buy my books." On the streets of Lagos, Nigeria, children are seen selling everything from chewing sticks to chocolate, many trying to earn money to pay for books. Most of Africa is part of the Third World, which contains masses of people who eke out a precarious existence on incomes of less than two hundred pounds per year. Although money is scarce, in most homes education and books rank second only to food in the order of priority needs. It is hoped that one will never have to be sacrificed for the other.

Ladies and Gentlemen, I have a dream. That dream is that in the next ten years, every African child who is sixteen years of age will be not just literate, but a reader.

References

1. BASCOM, WILLIAM R., and MELVILLE J. HERSKOVITS. *Continuity and Change in African Cultures*. Chicago: University of Chicago Press, Phoenix Books, 1959.
2. BRYANT, JOHN. *Health and the Developing World*. Ithaca, New York and London: Cornell University Press, 1969.
3. DIKE, V.W. "School Library As a Tool for Developing Good Reading Habits in Children," paper presented to school librarians at the Alvan Ikoku College of Education, 1976.
4. ERIKEN, F., F.N. MBAJIORGU, E.A. NDIONU, and P.O. ONWULBIKO. "The Need for Adult Literacy in our Social Development," paper presented in partial fulfillment for the Award of the Nigerian Certificate of Education, Alvan Ikoku College of Education, Owerri, Nigeria, March 14, 1978.

5. FURTH, HANS G. *Piaget for Teachers.* Englewood Cliffs, New Jersey: Prentice-Hall, 1970.

6. IFEDI, CHUMA. "Birth Control: A Must," *Nigeria Daily Times,* March 15, 1978, 7.

7. JAHODA, GUSTAV. *The New Elites of Tropical Africa.* Barbara B. Lloyd, "Development of Class Identification among the Yoruba." London: Oxford University Press, 1966.

8. KENYATTA, JOMO. *Facing Mt. Kenya.* New York: Random House (Vintage Books), 1962, 96.

9. LERNER, DANIEL, and WILBUR SCHRAMM. *Communicaton and Change in the Developing Countries.* Honolulu, Hawaii: University Press, 1972.

10. MIDDLETON, JOHN, and GREET KERSHAW. *The Kikuyu and Kamba of Kenya.* London: International African Institute, 1972, 36.

11. MOORE, CLARK D., and ANN DUNBAR (Eds.). *Africa Yesterday and Today.* New York, Toronto, London: Bantam, 1968.

12. NJEMANZE, HAROLD K. "Red Trousers for Kawuba," an adaptation of a general English paper, Alvan Ikoku College of Education, Owerri, Nigeria.

13. NSUGBE, PHILIP O. *Ohaffia: A Matrilineal Ibo People.* New York: Oxford University Press, 1974.

14. NWAGWU, N.A. *U.P.E.: Issues, Prospects and Problems.* Benin City, Nigeria: Ethiope Press, 1976, 9.

15. RICHARDS, REGINA G. "Singing: A Fun Route to a Second Language," *Reading Teacher,* 29, 3 (December 1975), 283-284.

16. SHORTER, AYLWARD. *African Culture and the Christian Church.* London: Geoffrey Chapman, 1973, 165.

17. SHORTER, AYLWARD. *East African Societies.* London: Routledge and Kegan Paul, 1974.

18. SKINNER, ELLIOT P. *African Urban Life.* Princeton, New Jersey: Princeton University Press, 1974, 197.

19. STANISLOW, ANDRESKI. *The African Predicament.* New York: Atherton, 1968.

20. UDE, AGWU UDE. Third year student of Primary Education, Alvan Ikoku College of Education, Owerri, Nigeria, his comment.

21. UKEJE, B.O. "Igbo Concept of Family," address delivered in a symposium organized by Imo State Ministry of Education and Information, Cultural Division February 18, 1977, Owerri, Nigeria.

Opportunities to Use Family Resources for Reading in Developing Countries of Southeast Asia

Yaakub bin Karim
Ministry of Education
Kuala Lumpur
Malaysia

"Why can't Johnny read?" has become a universal issue and it is not surprising that reading in its broader sense has attracted a number of professional academicians, including psychologists, linguists, and educators, as well as parents. Research reports on reading are numerous and voluminous. But the problems and searches for solutions to problems still continue. In recent years, there has been an intense interest in how to obtain parent involvement (directly or indirectly) for extending reading programs at home and at school. It seems reasonable to suggest that many parents can be real assets to reading programs. There is also clear evidence from various studies that parent involvement and participation in the school programs produce positive long range effects on children's academic achievement and performance in reading.

Some Causes of Inadequate Reading

In advanced countries such as the United States, parent involvement in school-related activities, particularly in reading programs, has occurred on a wide scale. It is not uncommon to see parents and teachers at a conference table discussing ways and means to improve children's skills and their enthusiasm for reading. Too often, this is not the case in the countries of Southeast Asia, where numerous educational problems have been created by a number of circumstances. The factors that seem to have caused the educational problems include an explosive growth of population, disparities in opportunities between urban and rural areas; shortages of facilities; poor teaching practices; lack of qualified teachers; high rates of illiteracy and school dropouts; and also social, political, and economic pressures.

In the context of educational development the problems of reading appear to be as challenging as they are numerous. They are difficult enough to solve when many parents and teachers look upon reading simply as word recognition in one language, but they are magnified many times when the national language of instruction differs from the linguistic heritage of most parents and children. When reading is regarded as a thinking process that is activated by visual symbols and other interrelated factors, the complexities of adequate instruction in a developing country become obvious.

Parent Involvement

Many parents, particularly those with the minimal level of basic education, have been willing to take a relatively passive role in the educational process, accepting any decision handed down by the educational authorities. In contrast, there have been some cases in which parents have worked closely with schools and the lines of communication have been open and effective. Too often, however, such open lines of communication are lacking, and active parent roles are often quite limited.

Parents are a tremendous resource that schools can utilize to a greater extent than they usually have. A school that works closely with parents will find that the school-community bond will be stronger and, more important, that the children will benefit greatly. This paper will concern itself with examining the possibility of using family resources to help develop the reading skills of children in Southeast Asia. Since the paper is somewhat exploratory in nature and limited in scope, the references made to one country may not necessarily be fully applicable to other countries within the region. However, there are similarities as well as variations in many countries' educational systems, levels of development, and cultural-political history. For example, all the countries in this region are firmly committed to the goal of six to nine years of education for all children beginning at age six or seven. Despite the diversity of political situations and specific educational policies, there appears to be a core of common needs and problems that make it possible to discuss the opportunities to use family resources for reading as a broad regional concern.

The Language Problem

Before discussing reading further, it is necessary to look briefly at each country's common problems concerning the national language issue and the divergent linguistic backgrounds of children and their parents. In all Southeast Asian countries, at the first level of education, more than one language is taught. In countries such as Indonesia, Malaysia, Thailand, and Burma, although the population is comprised of several linguistic groups, the primary medium of instruction is a single national language. In Indonesia, the Bahasa Indonesia is used; in Thailand, the Thai language; and in Burma, the Burmese language. In spite of this national language policy, there is equal provision for children to learn their native or vernacular language in school. But usually a mismatch exists between the language taught in school and the language spoken at home. These language differences may tend to limit the parents' efforts in trying to help their children read. Obviously some parents may not have acquired the necessary second language skills at a level needed for effective intervention in children's reading instruction. This situation is even more difficult if such parents are illiterate or if their perception of reading is very limited. But within the family there may be some other adults who might be able to help— aunts, uncles, or adult siblings who have attained higher levels of education than that of the parents.

Books and Folklore

The contributions of adults cannot be directly associated with the reading activity but rather with providing a reading environment. This may include buying reading materials, telling the children stories based on their own experiences, interacting with the children in a more relaxed and comfortable manner, or just encouraging them to use the school and public libraries more extensively. In very remote rural areas, where such facilities are not available, parents can motivate children by showing an interest in their school work. Parents should ask their children what they have learned in school and perhaps try to develop some form of related learning tasks for the children at home. The parents can give the children some time for study rather than asking them to engage in tasks which are not related to the children's school work.

Most parents, especially in Malaysia, are familiar with folktales and other forms of oral literature. They can tell stories such as that of the "San Kangil" (The Shrewd Mousedeer) who outwits the lion, the tiger, the elephant, and the crocodile every time but who is, in just one instance, outmatched by the stork. Everybody knows that young children like stories about animals, adventures, and funny situations. Stories such as "The Adventures of Hang Tuah", a famous Malay warrior in the Fifteenth Century, still are popular among the community, even though they could view these stories in a more critical way. Other stories like "Musang Berjanggut," "Lebai Malang," "Si-Luncai," and "Pak Kaduk" are among the most popular ones. Besides instilling reading interest through storytelling, parents can inculcate moral development. Stories such as "Ramayana," from Sanskrit literature, have been translated into the Malaysian national language (Bahasa Malaysia) and other available literature is written in different languages, particularly in English. Because of the technological developments, many of these pieces of literature have been put into print, but in research on Malay literature many of the old stories have been retrieved through oral interviews with field workers and village elders (kampungs). Thus, in Malaysia the parents have abundant resources that can be tapped and utilized much more extensively than usual. The situation presumably is the same in other countries in the region. Even if the parents in any area may be termed illiterate in a strict sense of the word, educators should not overlook their capacity to tell or recite stories, especially those that possess historical significance or the qualities of folklore.

Radio, Television and other Mass Media

Researchers have recognized that mass media can function to advance reading. In a recent study, Katni (6) questioned a sample of 500 parents, finding that 36.6 percent read newspapers in the National language. Among the younger parents with English education backgrounds, however, 70.6 percent read the newspapers in the English language. The sample in this study was quite representative of the whole population because it took into account the rural population distribution pattern of the country. It provided clear evidence that newspapers are one of the most popular reading materials of the adult population, probably because they are sold at a very low price compared with other journals and periodicals.

Clearly, if parents read newspapers regularly, it is also possible that these materials can be utilized for the development of childhood reading skills. Strategies can be planned to lead children to notice and recognize key words in newspaper headlines and to listen to parents reading parts of some news stories aloud. In situations where newspapers cannot be purchased because of limited funds, community centres can provide such materials. Then the parents can encourage their children to utilize the facilities available in such centres.

The number of books in the home might not always determine whether a child is a good reader or a poor reader, but research evidence supports the idea that good readers generally have more books and reading materials at home. Likewise, more emphasis is given to education in homes where children are the good readers. This seems to prove that the home environment greatly influences children's reading habits and abilities. In the absence of books and other reading materials, it is possible for parents to take alternative steps. For instance, the use of mobile libraries and community centres can be encouraged. In developing countries, however, such services are provided on a limited basis. This is particularly true in Malaysia, about which Nadarajah (11) said that, "Although library development has been phenomenal ... the development of libraries is only incidental and did not come about as government priority." Still, it is encouraging to note that in spite of the continuing shortage of reading materials, much effort is being made by all sectors concerned, and there has been consistent improvement during the past decade or two.

Because of the presence of a television set in nearly every home, parents can hardly ignore this medium as a means of supporting learning. "Out-of-school" viewing can involve parents with their children. In situations where television sets are not available in the home, sets usually are found in the community centres. Rather than allowing the children to view programs entirely by themselves, parents can help guide their children to view some of the programs that are educational in nature and to discuss what they see. The radio, too, can function as an educational resource in the sense that it supplies useful language experiences as well as information on civilization and social science. By listening to the radio, children can develop and sharpen their listening skills. Some educational radio programs are especially designed for children as a supplement to school learning tasks. Parents can help their children use such programs in a purposeful and effective way.

Parent Education to Improve Reading Instruction

Adult education has been regarded as a logical way to supply systematic guidelines to parents in helping their children improve reading skills. One of the main objectives of such parent education is to acquaint parents with the simple reading skills that they can reinforce by practice at home. A major difficulty in this approach is encountered in trying to maintain a high level of consistent parent participation, especially in the rural areas. To date, it has been difficult to get parents fully involved in these programs. All parents can see that their children do their homework, get enough sleep, and get proper food, but to get the children involved directly in the reading program is another matter. For this they need basic principles of child psychology and demonstrations of teaching techniques. Those who are interested can be exposed to many essential ideas through classroom meetings, visits to classes, workshops, and discussions.

Conclusion

The improvement of reading cannot be achieved by a few administrative decisions, nor in the adoption of one set of teaching methods to the exclusion of others. Improvement will come about only from a thorough understanding of the many complexities related to reading; such action must be taken on a broad front. While most Southeast Asian countries are experiencing political and social changes, there are opportunities to begin using family resources to improve reading capability. As the Bullock Report (7) suggests, improvement in the teaching of reading will come only from a comprehensive study of all the factors at work and by the influence that can be exerted upon them. Currently much government activity is directed toward seeking new alternatives to provide universal basic education for the people, especially to provide programs which increase educational opportunities for the "poor." Attempts have been made to improve the quality of teaching in primary schools and to make primary schools more relevant to the developmental needs of the country. This effort has given rise to problems of resources (teacher shortages, underqualified teachers, unavailability of books and related reading materials, lack of adequate facilities, and supplies, and other infrastructural variables). These and similar problems stem from the rapid changes in the economic and social structures, which gave priority to the acquisition of academic and vocational skills.

Involvement of parents in the development of reading programs usually has not been seen as part of the ordinary educational procedures. Parents sometimes have participated in parent-teacher organizations and have had occasional meetings with classroom teachers and other school personnel. Their role in such meetings often is concerned with general matters such as discipline, absenteeism, or textbooks which the children have purchased. Usually the participation of parents, businesses, and the community in general is greatly encouraged. To a considerable extent community leaders and parents have joined hands and contributed their labour, money, and materials for school building construction (5). This clearly indicates that parents who are given the opportunity for continuous and vigorous participation, particularly in the reading programs, can contribute to significant progress in reading. Through adult education programs, for instance, much effort could be channeled toward reading objectives. Parents' attitudes, aspirations, and interests could be built if school professionals would work cooperatively to establish better understanding and communication. The task is a difficult one, but greater success can be anticipated.

To sum up the discussion, it is my belief that children's reading performance can be improved when the parents share responsibility with school personnel and when family resources are fully utilized. This is not always possible because of the language limitations and the economic pressures parents have to overcome. In some cases, because of their extreme poverty, some of their children have not yet enrolled in the regular school. But regardless of how or where reading is taught, parents can always be considered important contributors toward their children's success.

References

1. ANCHOR, KENNETH N., and FELICIA N. ANCHOR. "School Failure and Parental Involvement in an Ethnically Mixed School: A Survey," *Journal of Community Psychology*, 2 (July 1974), 265-267.
2. DOWNING, JOHN. *Comparative Reading: Cross-National Studies of Behavior and Process in Reading and Writing*. New York: Macmillan, 1973.
3. *Education in Asia*. Bulletin of the Unesco Regional Office for Education in Asia, 6 (2), 1-X (1972), 11-24, 57-64, 89, 107, 115, 166, 181, 189, 209.
4. HEISLER, FLORENCE, and FRANCIS CRAWLEY. *Parental Participation: Its Effects on the First Grade Achievement of Children in a Depressed Area*. Albany, New York: Eric Document Reproduction Service ED 0392651.
5. HUSIN, A. *Innovation in the Management of Primary School Construction in Indonesia: A Case Study*. Unesco Regional Office for Education in Asia and Oceania, 1977, 9.
6. KATNI, KIBAT B. "Reading Habits and Interests of the Rural Malays: A Methodological Study," unpublished doctoral dissertation, University of Pittsburgh, 1978.
7. *A Language for Life*. Report by a Committee of Inquiry appointed by the Secretary of State of Education and Science under the Chairmanship of Sir Alan Bullock, FBA, HMSO, 1975.
8. LOBAN, W. *The Language of Elementary School Children*. Urbana, Illinois: National Council of Teachers of English, 1963.
9. McCORMICK, SANDRA. "Should You Read Aloud to Your Children?" *Language Arts*, 2, 54 (February 1977), 139-143, 163.
10. MITLER, WILMA H. "Home Prereading Experiences and First Grade Reading Achievement," *Reading Teacher*, 22, 7 (April 1969), 641-645.
11. NADHARAJAR, RADHA. "Education for Librarianship in Malaysia: Its History and Development and Comparison with Developments in Indonesia."
12. NIEDERMEYER, FRED C. "Parents Teach Kindergarten Reading at Home," *Elementary School Journal*, May 1970, 438-445.

13. SCHIFF, HERBERT J. "The Effect of Personal Contractual Relationships on Parent's Attitudes toward and Participation in Local School Affairs," *Dissertation Abstracts*, 25 (1964), 202-203.
14. STRICKLAND, R. "The Language of Elementary School Children," *Bulletin of School of Education, Indiana University*, 38 (1962).

Family Forces for Preschool Development of Health, Vocabulary, and Perceptual Skills

Betty Horodezky
University of British Columbia
Vancouver, British Columbia
Canada

Historical Prospective

It seems ironic that man, despite his intellectual prowess and esteemed place in the hierarchy of the animal kingdom, has found that his greatest challenge remains not in conquering space nor in perfecting technology, but in providing for the optimum educational needs of his young.

This challenge has not gone unnoticed in the past, and we cannot claim that early education or readiness is a recent innovation. A review of history will reveal that educators have sought for centuries to expand their knowledge of preschool experiences which foster learning (1).

As early as 1657, Comenius proposed that a Mother's School be established in every home for every child during the first six years of life; perhaps even more impressive was his proposal that prenatal education be provided for mothers (17).

Writings by Rousseau in 1762, showed further progress toward the concept of readiness and early education. This was exemplified in his book *Emile*, where he underscored the need for providing for education through a series of developmental stages from birth through early adulthood (17).

Early in the nineteenth century, Froebel's writings,

influenced by those of Rousseau and Pestalozzi, stressed a strong need for reform in educating the young. His ideas on the educational value of play were to be reflected later in the practices of the first kindergartens in Europe and the United States.

These are but a few of the well known educators from our historic past who sought to improve the educational environment for the vast numbers of children of the poor in Europe. In their writings, one can see the first appearance of the concepts of preschool education, readiness, and family involvement—not too unlike our present day educational theories.

In America, the concerns for additional changes in early education were not felt until the Sputnik era of the 1950s and the 1960s. At this time, it was found that large numbers of preschool children from impoverished homes were seriously lacking in the fundamental educational experiences needed for cognitive growth and success in school. Leading theorists— including Hunt, Bruner, and Bloom—espoused the importance of the child's early environment, and addressed attention to the "crucial" first five years of intellectual development.

In a concerted effort to stem public criticism of the excess failure rate in schools and to answer the need for equal educational opportunities for all segments of the population, federally funded programs such as Head Start were launched (17). The rapid expansion of these programs since the sixties has enjoyed continued support over the past two decades.

Although research reports on the success of programs have been inconclusive, it is encouraging to note that studies such as the Willmon investigation (33) of parent participation in Head Start programs, the Brzeinski experiment (2) in Denver, and the research by Durkin (11) have all reflected the potential of an active liaison between the school and home in better preparing preschool children in the tasks of getting ready to read.

The thesis of this paper thus lies not in *whether* parents should help their children, but in *why* parents should help their children in a "home start" effort geared toward fostering growth in prereading skills.

Influence of Health on Preschool Learning

If children are to be expected to grow and learn to their maximum abilities, they must possess good health and stimulating environments. Both mental and physical growth are dependent upon the kind of nutrition, environment, and physical hygiene children experience during their growing years (Brzeinski, 1964).

The negative effect of maternal malnutrition upon the mental and physical development of the unborn child has received considerable attention (23). Equally critical, and perhaps less well understood by parents and educators, is the negative effect of severe malnutrition on the physical and mental development of the newborn infant during the first few months of life. Research is now telling us that if infants are deprived of proper nutrition or stimulation during the first few years of life, there is a strong likelihood they will never reach their full physical and mental capacity (18).

In a summary of studies on the effect of malnutrition on development, Cravioto (5) said that "the existence of an association between protein calorie malnutrition in infancy and retardation in mental development has been established beyond reasonable doubt." Also, the mental lag incurred by severe malnutrition during the very early months in the infant's life may produce lasting consequences.

Similarly, the Dobbing and Sands study (9) on the effect of nutrition on brain development revealed that the most important growth spurt in brain development takes place after birth, not before birth as previously assumed, and rapid development continues for at least two years. The damaging effects of inadequate nutrition and stimulation during this critical time could be permanent (18). Eichenwald and Fry (13) suggest that starvation during the first six months of life is more likely to have profound and permanent effect upon the physical, intellectual, and emotional development of the individual than starvation after the second year of life.

In investigating whether severe malnutrition inflicted during the first few months of life can be reversed, Monckeberg (21) provided extended treatment for fourteen infants who had been afflicted with severe malnutrition during their first few months. His findings were that at three to six years of age, most of the children were at normal weight, were generally short for their age, and had an average IQ of 62—significantly below normal. Monckeberg concluded that the retarding effect of early severe malnutrition during the critical period of brain development is irreversible.

Although more definitive evidence is still needed on the relationship between early nutrition and brain development and mental ability, we do know that adequate nutrition is of prime importance to preschool children if they are to function as alert and responsive learners. Since the process of attaining reading competence begins essentially from the moment of conception rather than from the moment of entering school, and because reading involves the total growth of the child, it is imperative that parents and educators understand the implications of nutrition in providing for pre and postnatal care of the young.

Preschool Development: Vocabulary and Perceptual Skills

One of the unique characteristics of man is his "gift" of language (7). From the prelinguistic birth utterance to mature spoken language, verbal development takes on a sequential pattern; only under conditions of environmental or intellectual deprivation does this pattern vary (17).

Before entering school, children have already attained extensive practice in linguistic development from their home and community environments. With approximately six years of listening to language and five years of their own verbalization, children make significant progress toward mastering the structural patterns of language. At no other time will they accomplish such dramatic growth in language development as during these preschool years (7).

Since basic language is learned long before children come to school, the richness of their vocabulary and their language facility will be determined largely by the interest, attention, and communicative adult interaction they enjoy at home. Parent and sibling responses to children's vocal expressions are an essential component in children's early language development (8). The family not only provides the language model, but the kind of language children will ultimately imitate (25).

Cazden (4) found that children could make language gains if they were given an opportunity to interact with responsive adults. In this vein, Smith (28) observed that the speaking vocabularies of children from environments where speaking was not encouraged had vocabularies of as few as 500 words, while children from environments where verbal language was encouraged had vocabularies of approximately 2,500 words—a very significant difference.

The early development of auditory and visual discrimination as prereading skills is also of major importance. Studies by Harrington and Durrell (15) and by Nicholson (24) showed that factors of auditory and visual discrimination are of greater importance to reading readiness and reading achievement than mental age.

Because of all this research evidence, the Spaches (30) contend that children with exceedingly poor language development, meager vocabularies, poor articulation, and inadequate communicative skills, will undoubtedly have difficulty with reading.

It is, therefore, urgent for parents who are preparing children for reading to provide opportunities for developing prerequisite skills of: 1) being able to understand the multiple meanings of words; 2) being able to speak the language effectively; 3) being able to discriminate auditory and visual likenesses and differences in printed symbols and words; and 4) demonstrating perceptual motor skills related to direction—discriminating left from right, up from down, and page turning (29). Reading is a language process (16), and much of the children's success will depend upon varied early family activities because ". . . involving children in direct experiences helps to build a rich experiential background that is essential not only for sustaining interest, but also for building concepts, extending vocabulary, and establishing the rich oral language base necessary for a successful beginning in reading" (26).

Influence of Home Environment

During the 1930s and up to the 1960s, the school attitude toward parental participation in educating their children was generally one of "leave it to us"—it was preferred that parents not meddle in the "magic process" of teaching their children to read (*14*). In sharp contrast to this, the attitude that emerged over the 1960s and 1970s seemed to be reversed by asking the question, "What can we do to involve family forces in the process of preparing young children for reading?" (*14*).

Numerous authorities have commented on the importance of home environment to prereading development. Durkin (*11*) pointed out that the urgent need is to help parents realize the important differences between a home that is intellectually stimulating and one that is intellectually smothering."

Early studies by Brzeinski (*2*), Sheldon and Carrillo (*27*), and Sutton (*31*), revealed a significant relationship between children's home prereading experiences and later success in beginning reading. More recent studies by Vukelich (*32*), Criscuolo (*6*), and Woods (*34*) have lent additional support to the theory that knowledgeable parents can enhance their children's prereading skills.

Varying factors such as parental education, cultural interests, income, and family stability all affect the quantity and quality of reading development children will experience in their first learning environment—the home (*30*). Miller (*20*) identified some of the characteristics of the homes of deprived children as: 1) lacking in physical stimulation necessary for vocabulary and concept development, 2) being congested and having a high noise level, 3) encouraging sparse verbal communication between the preschool child and the parent, 4) revealing parent use of imprecise vocabulary, and 5) having an inadequate home schedule.

Numerous studies conducted in this area have concurred "...that social class greatly influences the kind of school performance the child will have" (*19*). However, one well might conjecture that educational poverty is not the inheritance of the poor only, for neither luxury nor poverty are necessary and sufficient conditions for determining the atmosphere for learning to read; "It is what the child experiences in the home and neighborhood that makes the difference" (*28:11*).

In conclusion, research has shown that, with proper guidance, parents can make a valuable contribution toward their children's initial experiences in learning to read" . . . if educational research in early childhood education is to have a major impact, it must include the added dimension of the home . . ." (2:240). As Montagu so aptly stated ". . . the most enduring of all tragedies for the child and his society lies in the difference between what he was capable of becoming, and what he has in fact been caused to become..." (13).

Suggested Publications and Materials

Preschool Preparation for Reading: Parents and Teachers

BIBLIOGRAPHIES
Honig, Alice Sterling (Compiler). *Language Learning, Language Development: A Bibliography.* ED 107 961
Quisenberry, Nancy L., Candace Blakemore, and Claudia A. Warren. "Involving Parents in Reading: An Annotated Bibliography," *Reading Teacher*, October 1977, 34-39.

PUBLICATIONS BY IRA AND ERIC/CRIER
Chan, Julie M.T. *Why Read Aloud to Children?* Newark, Delaware: International Reading Association, 1974.
Eberly, Donald W. *How Does My Child's Vision Affect His Reading?* Newark, Delaware: International Reading Association, 1972.
Smith, Carl B. (Ed.). *Parents and Reading.* Newark, Delaware, International Reading Association, 1971.
Rogers, Norma. *What Is Reading Readiness?* Newark, Delaware, International Reading Association, 1971.
Rogers, Norma. *How Can I Help My Child Get Ready To Read?* Newark, Delaware: International Reading Association, 1972.
Rogers, Norma. *What Books and Records Should I Get for My Preschooler?* Newark, Delaware: International Reading Association, 1972.

BROCHURES FOR PARENTS
Published by the International Reading Association
P.O. Box 8139, 800 Barksdale Road
Newark, Delaware 19711
Your Home Is Your Child's First School
You Can Encourage Your Child to Read
Reading and Prefirst Grade

PAMPHLETS AND BOOKLETS
Bayless, Nancy, and others. *Help! What Can I Do with My Four Year Old?* Wamego, Kansas: Kaw River Valley Special Education Co-op Reading Teachers, 1975. (Discusses aspects of health and auditory and visual discrimination.)
How Parents Can Help and What They Can Do At Home. Millville, Utah: Home Start Training Centre (3 pages of ideas).
Johnson, Ferne. *Start Early for an Early Start.* ALA, 1976.
Language Experiences for Your Preschooler Part I: Activities at Home. Albany: State University of New York, Department of Education, Bureau of

Continuing Education Curriculum Development (25 pages of excellent activities).
Reading Begins at Home. Field Enterprises Educational Corporation and American Library Association, no date.

PERIODICALS FOR PARENTS

Growing Child. Published by Dunn and Hargitt, Learning Laboratory, Indiana University, Lafayette, Indiana. (Monthly newsletter for young parents. Suggestions for rearing and educating children from birth to five years of age.) $5.95 a year.

Learning Child. 124 W. State Street, West Lafayette, Indiana 47902. $2 a year.

BOOKS

Clark, Margaret. *Young Fluent Readers: What Can They Teach Us?* London: Heinemann Educational Books, 1976.

Dodson, Fitzhugh. *How to Parent.* Los Angeles, Nash Publishing, 1970. (Suggestions for assisting children in developing emotional and intellectual maturity.)

McDiarmid, Norma J., Mari A. Peterson, and James R. Sutherland. *Loving and Learning.* Don Mills: Longman Canada Ltd., 1975. (Surveys each age category and gives suggestions for concept development and reading activities for parents.)

White, Burton R. *Experience and Environment: Major Influence on Development of Young Children,* Vol. 1. Englewood Cliffs, New Jersey: Prentice-Hall, 1973.

White, Burton R. *The First Three Years of Life.* Englewood Cliffs, New Jersey: Prentice-Hall, 1975.

HANDBOOKS

Ahr, Edward, and Benita Simons. *Parent Handbook.* Priority Innovations, Box 792, Skokie, Illinois 60076. $2.15.

Arbuthnot, May Hill. *Children's Reading in the Home.* Glenview, Illinois: Scott, Foresman, 1969.

Baratta-Lorton, Mary. *Workjobs for Parents.* Reading, Massachusetts: Addison-Wesley, 1975.

Cullinan, Bernice E., and Carolyn W. Carmichael (Eds.). *Literature and Young Children.* Urbana, Illinois: National Council of Teachers of English, 1977.

De Franco, Ellen B., and M. Pickarts. *Dear Parents: Help Your Child to Read!* Cincinnati, Ohio: American Book. (Preschool-1, games and activities for home.) $1.17.

Forte, Imogene, and Joy Mackenzie. *Which Is the Way to Wednesday?* Nashville, Tennessee: Incentive Publications. (A book to help children understand the meaning of reading.)

Lally, J. Ronald. *Learning Games for Infants and Toddlers.* New Readers Press, Box 131, Syracuse, New York.

Larrick, Nancy. *A Parent's Guide to Children's Reading.* New York: Pocket Books, 1964.

McKee. *A Primer for Parents.* Boston, Massachusetts: Houghton Mifflin, 1971.

Parents as Resource. *Recipes for Fun.* English and Spanish editions. Par Project, 464 Central, Northfield, Illinois 60093. (Ages 2-7.) $2.

Parents as Resource. *More Recipes for Fun.* Par Project, 464 Central, Northfield, Illinois 60093. (Ages 3-11.) $2.

Health, Vocabulary, and Perceptual Skills   51

Reading: Success for Children Begins at Home. Home and School Institute, Box 4847, Cleveland Park, Washington, D.C. 20008. (Other useful materials also available.)

Scott, Ralph, Guy Wagner, and Joan Cesinger. *Home Start Ideabook.* Early Years Press, 1976.

Shakesby, Paul S. *Child's Work.* Philadelphia: Running Press, 1974.

Sparkman, Brandon, and Jane Saul. *Preparing Your Preschooler for Reading: A Book of Games.* New York: Schocken Books, 1977. (Visual and listening games.)

Stein, Sara Bonnett. *New Parents' Guide to Early Learning.* New American Library, 1301 Avenue of the Americas, New York 10019. (Enrichment ideas for preschool children.) $3.95.

JOURNAL AND BOOK ARTICLES

Amselmo, Sandra. "Parent Involvement in the Schools," *Clearinghouse,* 50 (March 1977), 297-799.

Chomsky, Carol. "Stages in Language Development and Reading Exposure," *Harvard Educational Review,* 42 (February 1972), 1-33.

Foulks, Patricia. "How Early Should Language Development and Prereading Experiences Be Started?" *Elementary English,* 42 (1974), 310-315.

Freshour, Frank W. "Parents Can Help," *Reading Teacher,* March 1972, 513-516.

Gordon, Ira. "Present Involvement in Early Childhood Education," *National Elementary Principal,* 51 (1971), 26-30.

Johnson, Mary Frances K. "Creating a Good Reading Climate at Home," in Virginia H. Matthews (Ed.), *Parents and Beginning Reading.* Washington, D.C.: National Reading Centre, 1972. ED 064 705

Johnson, Marjorie S. "Reading Readiness: What Parents Should Know about It," in Virginia H. Matthews (Ed.), *Parents and Beginning Reading.* Washington, D.C.: National Reading Centre, 1972, 15-17. ED 064 705

Larrick, Nancy. "Reading Games to Play at Home" in Virginia H. Matthews (Ed.), *Parents and Beginning Reading.* Washington, D.C.: National Reading Centre, 1972, 7-8. ED 064 705

Pikulski, John J. "Parents Can Aid Reading Growth," *Elementary English,* 51 (September 1974), 896-897.

Stavitschek, Joseph J., and Alan Hofmeister. "Parent Training Packages," *Children Today,* March/April 1975, 23-25.

Swift Marshall S., and others. "Preschool Books and Mother-Child Communication," *Reading Teacher,* December 1971.

RESEARCH/ERIC DOCUMENTS

Durkin, Dolores. "A Six Year Study of Children Who Learned to Read in School at Age Four," *Reading Research Quarterly,* 10 (1974-1975), 9-61.

John, Vera. *Environmental Influences on Language Development.* ED 001 889

Jones, Pauline. *Home Environment and the Development of Verbal Ability.* ED 047 048

References

1. BROPHY, JERE E., L. THOMAS, and SHARI E. NEDLER. *Teaching in the Preschool.* New York: Harper and Row, 1975.

2. BRZEINSKI, JOSEPH E. "Beginning Reading in Denver," *Reading Teacher,* 18 (1964), 16-21.

3. BRZEINSKI, JOSEPH E., and WILL HOWARD. "Early Reading: How, Not When!" *Reading Teacher,* 25 (1971), 239.

4. CAZDEN, C. "Environmental Assistance to the Child's Acquisition of Grammar," unpublished doctoral dissertation, Harvard University, 1965.
5. CRAVIOTO, J. "Complexity of Factors Involved in "Protein-Calorie Malnutrition," in P. Gyorgy and O.L. Kline (Eds.), *Manhattan Is a Problem of Ecology*. Basel and New York: Karger 1970, 7,12,22.
6. CRISCUOLO, NICHOLAS P. "Parents: Active Partners in the Reading Program," *Elementary English*, 51 (1974), 883-884.
7. DALLMAN, MARTHA, and others. *The Teaching of Reading*. New York: Holt, Rinehart and Winston, 1978, 19, 25, 78.
8. DEVERELL, ALFRED E. *Teaching Children to Read and Write*. Toronto: Holt, Rinehart and Winston of Canada, 1973, 16-18.
9. DOBBING, J., and J. SANDS. "Timing of Neuroblast Multiplication in Developing Human Brain," *Nature*, 1970, 6-39.
10. DOWNING, JOHN, and DEREK THACKRAY. *Readiness*. Toronto: Hodder and Stoughton, 1976.
11. DURKIN, DOLORES. "Early Readers: Reflections after Six Years of Research," *Reading Teacher*, 18 (1964), 3-7.
12. DURKIN, DOLORES. "When Should Children Begin to Read?" in Helen M. Robinson (Ed.), *Innovation and Change in Reading Instruction, NYSSE*. Chicago: University of Chicago Press, 1968, 70.
13. EICHENWALD, H.F., and P.C. FRY. "Nutrition and Learning," *Science*, 163 (1969), 644-648.
14. FRY, EDWARD. *Elementary Reading Instruction*. New York: McGraw Hill, 1977, 125.
15. HARRINGTON, SISTER M.J., and D.D. DURRELL. "Mental Maturity versus Perception Abilities in Primary Reading," *Journal of Educational Psychology*, 46 (1955), 375-380.
16. HEILMAN, ARTHUR W. *Principles and Practices of Teaching Reading*. Columbus, Ohio: Charles E. Merrill, 1977.
17. LEEPER, SARAH HAMMOND, and others. *Good Schools for Young Children*. New York: Macmillan, 1974, 6-7, 174-175.
18. LEWIN, ROGER. "Starved Brains," *Psychology Today*, September 1975, 29-33.
19. MILLER, WILMA H. *The First R: Elementary Reading Today*. New York: Holt, Rinehart and Winston, 1972, 13.
20. MILLER, WILMA H. *Elementary Reading Today*. New York: Holt, Rinehart and Winston, 1972, 41.
21. MONCKEBERG, F. "Mental Retardation from Malnutrition: Irreversible . . .," *Journal of the American Medical Association*, 206 (1968), 30-31.
22. MONROE, MARION, and BERNICE ROGERS. *Foundations for Reading*. Glenview, Illinois: Scott, Foresman, 1964, 172.
23. MONTAGU, ASHLEY. "Sociogenic Brain Damage," *American Anthropologist*, 74 (1972), 1045-1061.
24. NICHOLSON, A. "Background Abilities Related to Reading Success in First Grade," *Journal of Education*, 1958, 7-24.
25. PETTY, WALTER T., DOROTHY C. PETTY, and MARJORIE F. BECKING. *Experiences in Language*. Boston: Allyn and Bacon, 1973, 9.
26. SCHULWITZ, BONNIE S. "The Teacher Fostering Interest and Achievement," in Lloyd O. Ollila (Ed.), *The Kindergarten Child and Reading*. Newark, Delaware: International Reading Association, 1977, 46.
27. SHELDON, W. D., and L. W. CARRILLO. "Relation of Parents, Home, and Certain Developmental Characteristics to Children's Reading Ability," *Elementary School Journal*, January 1952, 262-270.
28. SMITH, CARL B. "The Effect of Environment on Learning to Read," in Carl B. Smith (Ed.), *Parents and Reading*. Newark, Delaware: International Reading Association, 1971, 11,13.

Health, Vocabulary, and Perceptual Skills

29. SMITH, RICHARD J., and DALE D. JOHNSON. *Teaching Children to Read.* Don Mills, Ontario: Addison-Wesley, 1976, 72.
30. SPACHE, GEORGE D., and EVELYN B. SPACHE. *Reading in the Elementary School.* Boston: Allyn and Bacon, 1977.
31. SUTTON, MARJORIE HUNT. "Readiness for Reading at the Kindergarten Level," *Reading Teacher*, 22 (1964), 234-239.
32. VUKELICH, CAROL. "Parents' Participation as a Factor in a Reading Readiness Program," unpublished manuscript, University of Delaware, 1977.
33. WILLMON, B. J. "Reading Readiness as Influenced by Parent Participation in Head Start Programs," in J. A. Figurel (Ed.), *Reading and Realism.* Newark, Delaware: International Reading Association, 1969, 617-622.
34. WOODS, CAROL, and others. *The Effect of the Parent Involvement Program on Reading Readiness Scores.* Mesa, Arizona: Mesa Public Schools, 1974.

Family Forces for Early School Development of Language Fluency and Beginning Reading

Mary McDonnell Harris
Kansas State University
Manhattan, Kansas
United States of America

This paper follows the preschool child, discussed by Dr. Horodezky, into the early school years. With school entry, the dyadic relationship between parent and child must admit a third actor, the teacher. As teachers assume major responsibility in children's academic development, they must seek the continuing partnership of parents for several reasons. First, parents *want to help* their children with reading at home. Second, parents *can help* children, often in ways that are difficult or impossible to carry out in the school environment.

Parental desire and ability to support the teaching of beginning reading are documented by recent studies. A 1977 Gallup poll reported virtually all United States parents receptive to involvement in the educational process. When Cassidy (5) asked parents of primary youngsters to rank facts about their children's reading progress in order of importance, "things parents can do to help children" ranked first. Studies of home involvement in reading programs demonstrate parental effectiveness as "volunteer" teachers of kindergarten and primary children under the guidance of regular teachers (*38, 44, 49*).

Family Activities Promote Reading

When teachers are able to respond to parents' queries about how to help their primary school children with reading, a partnership can be forged. The following suggestions for families were gleaned from over forty sources addressed to parents and teachers. They are followed by suggestions to teachers as they mobilize family forces for reading success in the early school years.

Developing Language Fluency

Reading and writing skills are built on a foundation of oral language. These suggestions promote fluency in the use of oral language.

1. *Encourage conversation in the home.* "When talk is rich in content, topics, anecdotes, sharing of opinions and experiences; when it is spoken in a variety of tones and verbally colorful and inventive, the child is being prepared for the possibility of learning" (7:302). Times when the family is gathered for meals, for travel, or for an evening together are occasions for conversation.
2. *Talk with children.* Explain what you are doing and why. Speak lovingly and naturally, responding to questions and encouraging discussion (43:8).
3. *Encourage children to talk by listening to them without interrupting or anticipating what will be said.* Ask questions if you do not understand. Encourage children to explain their responses rather than simply nodding or pointing (54). Grandparents often can be the best listeners.
4. *Help older children to value conversations with primary age brothers and sisters.* Let them know that you value their making time to talk with and listen to younger children (29:4).
5. *Set standards for speech in the home that will enable children to communicate easily outside the home.* Do not encourage alternative terminology for expressions that may not be understood by nonfamily members.
6. *Encourage play with puppets, dolls, dress-up clothes, play stores, medical kits, and telephones.* Dramatic play fosters talking in a variety of roles. Siblings can help here.
7. *Participate as a family in games that build verbal fluency.* Cumulative games such as "I'm Going on a Trip" or "I Went to the Supermarket" develop memory and sentence building skills (48:118). Guessing games such as "Twenty Questions"

apply language skills in a problem solving situation. Books which include games for developing language fluency include *Home Start Ideabook (51)* and *Games to Improve Your Child's English (25)*.

8. *Enjoy rhymes, riddles, poems, jokes, and songs as part of the family's oral tradition.* Elephant riddles, knock-knock jokes, and jumprope rhymes are part of the verbal heritage of childhood. Share this lore as opportunities arise.

9. *Participate in storytelling for family fun.* Tell stories of parents' childhoods and tales of real and imaginary pets (2:39). Tell ghost stories, folktales, animal tales, and adventure stories. Try add-on stories in which each family member stops at the exciting place for the contribution of the next storyteller. Use open-ended stories in which one person narrates a conflict situation and others propose alternative solutions (43:9). Invite relatives to tell stories of their childhood.

10. *Talk about books.* Look at books one page at a time, and discuss the pictures. Encourage retelling of familiar stories from the pictures, and stimulate oral reactions to wordless picture books. When reading aloud, pause sometimes to ask questions such as "And what do you think happened then?" or "What would you do if that happened to you?" (50:65).

11. *Take trips with your children.* Talk about your plans, discuss what you see, and recall the experience together. Repeat trips to places you visited during the preschool years. Children's interests change and there will be many new things to discuss. Participating in planning is an important part of trip-taking for primary children (50:129).

12. *When your child makes errors in speaking, correct them casually.* If you believe your child's speech development is unusually slow, consult the speech therapist at school. Ask for an appraisal of your child's progress and for suggestions of ways to help at home (43).

Promoting Interest in Reading

Of all the ways families can contribute to reading growth, those that promote interest in reading receive the most attention in resources addressed to parents. Perhaps this is the single most important area for family activity.

1. *Good books beckon to children.* Knowing their children better than anyone else, parents are in a good position to select books that will interest them. The things children like to do usually are accurate indicators of their reading interests. When children are forming new interests is a good time to secure related reading material (40:897). Be alert to children's interests, likes and dislikes, problems and concerns, and use this information in selecting books at the library or the bookstore (41:6).

2. *A personal library affords children a collection of books selected with their interests in mind.* Book ownership teaches care of books and the opportunity to enjoy favorite books again and again. Several families with children of various ages may wish to reduce the cost of personal libraries by exchanging books as they are outgrown (2:102). Some books are never outgrown, however. Birthdays and other special occasions may be marked by giving children books inscribed for remembering through the years (15:6).

3. *Suggestions on books for children are available.* Teachers and librarians can provide help in selecting classics appropriate for gift giving, but choosing just the right new book is sometimes difficult. Lists of current children's books for holiday giving are sometimes included in fall issues of women's magazines, news weeklies, and newspapers. The *New York Times* reviews children's books each January (21:125). The *Horn Book Magazine* and the *Bulletin of the Center for Children's Books* of the University of Chicago provide reviews on which selections may be used. The Children's Book Council, 67 Irving Place, New York, New York 10003; the American Library Association, 50 East Huron Street, Chicago, Illinois 60611; and the Superintendent of Documents, United States Government Printing Office, Washington, D.C. 20402 supply lists of good children's books on request.

4. *A child's library should be attractive and accessible to the user.* A shelf the child has helped build or paint adds to the value of the library for that child (8:3). Personal bookplates may serve to increase pride in ownership of books for some children.

5. *Regular visits to the local library or bookmobile supplement a personal collection.* Library books form new interests, add dimension to established interests, and expand interests in unexpected ways. Time for browsing through the children's collection enables even nonreading children to explore interests through book selection. Most of the books checked out of the library should be of the child's choice.

6. *Book Clubs are another source of books for children.* Information about the Scholastic Book Clubs (Lucky and Arrow Books for primary children) is available through the schools. These, and other clubs, provide selections of inexpensive paperback books on a monthly basis (*31*:200).

7. *Children can find interesting reading material in periodicals.* Magazines of interest to primary children include: *Highlights for Children, Jack and Jill, Children's Playmate, Cricket, Ranger Rick, Ebony, Jr.,* and *Stone Soup.*

8. *Reading aloud as a family fosters togetherness, builds memories, and promotes enjoyment of literature.* Family reading should be planned for times when children are rested and relaxed. Experts suggest that, to be effective, reading aloud should occur at least 60 minutes per week but usually not more than 30 minutes per day (*29*:8). Reading aloud should not be discontinued when children are able to read. Select books slightly above their reading levels or books they would not be likely to choose for themselves. Biography, poetry, and drama all have a place in family reading programs. A knowledge of family interests combined with ideas from librarians and booklists should suggest endless possibilities. Books with bibliographies for family reading include *A Parent's Guide to Children's Reading (31)* and *Preparing Your Child for Reading (50).* *Let's Read Together: Books for Family Enjoyment* may be ordered from the American Library Association for $2 (*32*).

9. *Stories written by family members provide unique reading experiences.* Occasionally write a story featuring the adventures of family members in a real or imaginary situation (*41*). Grandparents will be pleased to write stories

of experiences from bygone days.

10. *Dictated stories are excellent material for reading aloud or for initial reading practice.* "Print" your children's stories as they dictate to you. Read back what has been written. Children may wish to illustrate their stories and save them to be reread later. Family albums, photographs, and scrapbooks are good stimuli for such dictation.

11. *Young children often enjoy hearing favorite stories read more frequently than adults enjoy reading them.* Records and cassette tapes of stories provide for unlimited retellings. Secure quality records and tapes for listening. Some sound tracks are designed so children may follow along in a companion book. In a few communities, Dial-a-Story enables children to hear stories (a different one each week) over the telephone (17:105).

12. *Take advantage of literary experiences provided for children by television and commercial films.* View literature based series, specials, or films together as a family, taking time to discuss them and comparing them with the related books when appropriate (46).

13. *Seek out community activities that promote books or foster literary appreciation.* Libraries may provide afterschool storyhours and films, book lists, and summer reading programs. Schools or community organizations may sponsor book displays, book fairs, or book exchanges. A government program, Reading is FUNdamental, supplies matching funds to groups who will raise money to give away children books. In some communities, children's theater introduces literature in a new dimension (47:20).

14. *Families who enjoy literature can find many ways to review and celebrate good books.* Role play scenes from favorite books, play charades based on book titles, or invent games that feature matching authors, titles, main characters, and plots (41). Poetry reading and recitation of frequently repeated poems contribute to the lives of families who have tuned into literature.

15. *Children's literature is not the only source of material that can intrigue beginning readers.* Magazines, newspapers, cartoons, game directions, labels on food containers, bulletin boards, street signs, and any other material read

by adults may have potential for interesting children in reading. Share whatever you are reading with children when they express interest (52:745).

16. *Use reference books to answer questions as they arise in the home.* The sight of adults looking things up in a dictionary, atlas, encyclopedia, thesaurus, concordance, or almanac teaches children the value of these books. Keep reference books in an accessible, well-lighted place where they can be easily used by children (31:129).

17. *A television guide is the most frequently used reference in many households.* Involve children in planning family television viewing schedules for the week. Over a period of time, family members can develop criteria to guide television program selection. Television can serve to broaden interests when viewing time is intentionally limited and when there is opportunity to discuss what has been viewed (54:17).

Fostering Independent Reading

Although reading can be shared by a group, it is usually pursued independently. A child's reading skills develop with independent practice. The habits of independent reading established in childhood enrich the rest of a person's life. The suggestions in this section nurture independent reading.

1. *Independence in reading is fostered by adult models* (33:18). Seeing parents read in a variety of situations reinforces concepts of the uses and value of reading.

2. *Children who are gaining reading skills often want listeners.* Listen to children read to share delight in their progress or to enjoy the story, not to offer corrections. Praise your child's reading judiciously, noting particular strengths (48:121). The story may be too simple to elicit much substantive reaction but comment on the content, if possible, perhaps by relating it to the child's experiences.

3. *When asked, help your child with unknown words.* If the child seems receptive, you may ask "How does it start?" or "What would make sense?" to guide independent word attack (37:109). The child's teacher can suggest specific strategies for helping children approach unknown words.

4. *Books for independent reading should be at a level of difficulty comfortable for children.* Parents need to understand the difference between instructional and independent reading levels. This will help them appreciate why the materials used for independent reading should be less difficult than the basal reader used for instruction. Generally, children should miss no more than one word in twenty. A third grade teacher recommends to parents "the dirty thumb rule." Have the children count the unknown words on a page on the fingers of one hand. If the thumb is counted, the book is too hard (*39*). This rule works best for third graders because their books have about one hundred words per page.

5. *For the beginning reader, a major purpose of independent reading is to provide practice.* Reading many books at approximately the same level of difficulty reinforces skills, develops fluency, and builds confidence (*2:82*). A family's patience with easy-to-read materials helps children outgrow them. Among the series of good books for beginning readers are *I Can Read Books* (Harper and Row), *Let's Read and Find Out* books (Crowell), and *The True Book* Series (Children's Press) (*43*). The librarian can recommend others.

6. *Independent readers should have their own library cards, the right to choose library books, and the responsibility of caring for and returning books on time* (*14:515*). Wise selection of library books can be encouraged by teaching children to check readability and interest. Scanning the pictures or the text can help children to decide whether a book would be interesting enough to read or hear someone else read (*41:7*).

7. *Families can share times for independent reading.* SQUIRT (Sustained Quiet Reading Time), when everyone sits down with a book or periodical, provides a structure (*35:655*). The family may sometimes come together to read excerpts or talk about the contents of their individual reading selections.

8. *Independent reading can be fostered by notes and messages left at home or placed in a child's lunchbox.* One mother found that a posted dinner menu was favorite reading matter for her children (*4:188*). Notes telling where a snack may be found are invariably read. Children who regularly receive notes soon begin to write back.

9. *Writing is closely related to reading.* Materials for writers should be available in the home: pencils and markers, lined paper, note paper and envelopes, even a typewriter (*20*:5). Encourage the writing of lists, letters, and greeting cards. If a child asks how to spell a word, printing the word on a piece of paper to be copied will provide a visual image and reinforce reading skills.

10. *Everyday experiences can provide opportunities to practice reading skills.* Before a trip to the grocery store, children may help make shopping lists, examine newspaper ads, and clip coupons. At the store, beginning readers may be sent to find specific brands and types of food, refer to the store directory, compare prices, and check the cash register slip. Trips to service stations, post offices, restaurants, and movies afford similar opportunities (*28*).

11. *Cooking provides strong incentives for independent reading.* Children who have been taught to use kitchen utensils and appliances can follow simple recipes by themselves.

12. *Planning and taking a trip can lead to the reading of maps, travel guides, brochures, menus, billboards, and bumper-stickers (26:11).*

13. *Independent reading does not foster reading growth when the material read is too difficult or of little interest.* For this reason, parents may sometimes decide that reading content area textbooks aloud to their children is the best approach to homework assignments (*40*:897).

14. *When your child is looking for something to show and tell at school, suggest a favorite book (31:56).*

Parents Support School Efforts

Learning about Reading

The direct teaching of reading at school and in the home is a concern of many parents. Suggestions in this section are directed toward parents who feel they need to become involved in reading instruction.

1. *The teaching of reading is a popular topic for books and articles.* Adults must be critical readers of such materials. Authors whose suggestions are based on limited experience or who seem interested in "selling" a method should be studied with extreme caution. The cost efficiency of sugges-

tions, both in time and in money, should be considered. Some very effective methods of teaching reading consume more time and money than most people have (1:96).

2. *Most schools are eager to provide parents with overviews of the reading instructional program and with suggestions for helping readers at home.* Open houses, PTA meetings, or parent-teacher conferences may provide familiarity with the school reading program. If such meetings are not planned, request them, and ask for information on the best way to help your child at home. Knowing about the school reading program helps parents set realistic goals for their children (36:68).

3. *Many school districts are providing parents with booklets of suggestions for families.* These may be related to the reading levels of the school program or to the results of informal diagnostic procedures. *Help Your Child Learn to Read (13)* and *For Parents and Children: A Guide for Better Reading (20)* offer diagnostic tools and home activities, along with suggestions for coordinating them with the school program.

4. *Games and learning kits to supplement school instruction are provided for home use by some schools.* Ask your child's teacher about them.

5. *Parents and teachers may come together for informal discussions of experiences encountered as they work with children.* Through sharing, parents often find that their child's reading errors are characteristic of beginning readers and no cause for great concern (4).

6. *Some television programs, such as Sesame Street and The Electric Company, are designed to teach reading related skills.* Watching them may supplement and reinforce school or home instruction.

7. *Many toys and games are marketed through their alleged value in teaching reading.* Consumers should be cautious. If a toy would not be fun for children or if its advertising makes unrealistic promises, don't buy it. Many common family games have potential for reinforcing reading skills. Consider playing *Lotto, Bingo, Scrabble for Juniors, Anagrams, Word Roll,* or *Scribbage.*

8. *Teaching the alphabet is the first direct reading task under-taken by many parents.* This can be accomplished naturally and without pressure by searching for letters on signs or license plates and naming the letters in alphabet soup, cereals, and cookies. Children may make letters from pipe cleaners or clay, circle letters they recognize in newspapers or magazines, spell words with magnetic letters, or type letters on a typewriter (3:16). When playing alphabet games with children, parents should be aware of the complications presented by upper and lowercase letter forms. Emphasis on lowercase letters in manuscript print is recommended in the beginning; capitals come later.

9. *A repertory of sight words can be developed through home activities.* Parents may introduce new words by placing labels on foods, furniture, toys, or clothing. The child shows recognition of words by placing them by the appropriate objects (29:8). New words may be displayed in the child's room on a mobile or placed on cards for use in games such as *Concentration, Go Fish,* and *Rummy.* Searches for known words may be conducted in the newpaper or on sign-boards viewed from an automobile. The possibilities for enjoyable word drills are endless. One parent printed new words on foam rubber cubes so his child could dive for them in the swimming pool (4).

10. *Word attack skills are developed through awareness of letter sounds and of which words make sense in the context of the passage.* Awareness of sounds can be cultivated by collecting word groups that alliterate, rhyme, or have the same number of syllables. Compound words, words with a common root, and homophones are fun to collect. Construct silly sentences or tongue twisters from the words collected (9:121). Appropriate activities are suggested in books by Forgan (13) and Granowsky, Middleton, and Mumford (20). Awareness of context can be developed through guessing games. For example, the parent may substitute "blank" for a key word in a passage, and the child may try to guess the missing word.

11. *Being able to follow verbal directions is important to a child's success in group reading instruction.* Give your

child practice in following oral and written directions. Playing games such as *Simon Says, Mother May I?* and *Upset the Fruit Basket* provides practice in following and remembering directions (*43*:11).

12. *At school, children are often expected to respond in writing.* Many beginning readers do not have the fine motor skills needed for writing. Games like *Jacks* and *Pick-Up-Sticks* and activities such as drawing, painting, cutting, and pasting help develop small muscles (*3*:18).

13. *Involvement is important in developing reading skills.* Parents can find reading practice procedures that will be fun for their children. An adult may read alternate pages with a practicing reader (*23*:56) or the two may read together as one points to the word being read (*24*:298). Younger siblings may be involved by having simple stories read by a beginner who has previously practiced. Placing stickers on a calendar provides incentive for daily practice in some families (*12*:182).

14. *Offer specific praise for oral reading strengths.* These may include trying to attack hard words, reading with expression, changing voices or styles for the speech of characters, or making a smooth transition from one page to another (*48*:121).

15. *Silent reading should be practiced, also.* Provide a time and quiet place. Tell words when asked, and discuss the material read by asking casual questions or listening to a retelling. While listening, focus full attention on the child.

16. *A variety of reading skills is needed for survival in today's world.* Reading telephone directories, address books, catalogs, directions on kits, labels on medicine containers, thermometers, globes, maps, and recipes all require specialized skill and practice. Survival reading situations are more often encountered in the home than in school. Thus, showing children how to use survival materials appropriate to their levels and providing practice situations for them is an especially good home reading activity. When practice experiences involve real life problems, children have little difficulty becoming interested in learning (*6*).

17. *Parents may receive periodic information on ways to form home-school partnerships for reading instruction by be-*

coming parent members of IRA. A newsletter for parents is also available from The Home and School Institute, Trinity College, Washington, D.C. 20017.

Creating a Climate for Learning

Learning is facilitated when the home and school work together and have confidence in one another. The suggestions in this section are directed toward parents concerned with creating an emotional climate in which children may learn to read successfully.

1. *Instill in your child an image of the school as a place to learn interesting things.* Display confidence that the child will learn there (*30:2*).
2. *Show your regard for the child's school involvement.* Attend school functions, visit the teacher, and find concrete ways to support the school program. Make a concerted effort to meet your child's teacher early in the school year (*42:725*).
3. *Avoid applying labels such as "dyslexic," "perceptually handicapped," or "underachieving," to your child.* Low expectations for a child's achievement can become self-fulfilling prophecies (*27:34*). Assume your child is working to capacity (*45:8*).
4. *Be sensitive to your child's individual style of learning.* When talking with others, do not compare your child with brothers, sisters, or neighborhood children. Such comparisons are unfair to the individuals involved and are likely to be reported to your child.
5. *Talk with your child about feelings.* Be alert to signals of pleasure, tiredness, or discouragement and talk about them (*30:3*).
6. *Provide a quiet place for your child to rest, think, and work alone.* The school environment is often lacking in privacy.
7. *Show interest.* Ask what your child has done in school and look with interest at what is brought home (*23*).
8. *Recognize that learning to read is sometimes frustrating.* Parents may be able to get in touch with feelings of beginning readers by relearning to read using the *Primer for Parents* (*34*). Help your child learn to deal with frustrations by talking about them.

9. *Help your child come to view mistakes as bases for learning.* Talk about your own mistakes and what you have learned from them.
10. *Teach your child to accept responsibility.* Do not do for children things they can do for themselves (26:26). Give children daily responsibilities they can handle (37:110).
11. *Discipline your child only when necessary.* Do not fall into a pattern of criticizing, nagging, or scolding (43:14).
12. *Discuss parenting dilemmas with other adults.* Lonely parents seem most likely to be unhappy with themselves and their children. Support yourself as a parent by attending meetings such as those organized for Parent Effectiveness Training (19).
13. *Do not use reading activities as bribes, threats, or punishments* (26:11). Exploited in such ways, reading takes on negative associations for the child.
14. *Let your child participate in community and school reading programs that offer rewards such as certificates or books.* Participating in a community reward system may be more effective than offering rewards for reading within the family, because the child is less likely to feel manipulated by the parents (4:190).
15. *Avoid giving the impression that children should do as you say, not as you do.* Reading together as a family makes each member a participant in an activity which is its own reward.

Teachers Offer Leadership
Suggestions for Teachers

As teacher's become aware of the many ways families can foster reading success during children's early school years, they must seek means of sharing instruction activities with parents. The following suggestions are addressed to teachers.

1. *Hold inservice meetings for parents.* Share information about the developmental reading program of the school, providing time to examine materials and to discuss parents' questions (53:788). Assess aspects of the reading program of most concern to families and plan followup meetings around them (22:713).

2. *Conduct workshops at which parents can make reading games and activities for family use* (9:121). Announcements sent out prior to the workshop may include lists of materials parents can provide or a pretest to help the parent determine which of the available activities would most help the child (6:639).
3. *Avoid educational jargon in contacts with parents.* Invitations to participate in reading-related activities must neither overly alarm the parent nor allow the family to underestimate its influence on children (12:181).
4. *Consider carefully the times and places of meetings with family members.* In some situations, homes or community buildings may be better meeting places than schools (35:654). Child care may be desirable. Repeated sessions on the same topic, but at different times, may accommodate a variety of parent work schedules or allow make-up of missed meetings.
5. *Share with parents the results of research which suggest differences between the family involvements of good and poor readers.* George (*18*) found that the reading aloud of books and stories, the availability of reading material for adults, and children's use of paper and pencils differentiated the homes of good from poor fifth grade readers. Parents of good readers differed from parents of poor readers in their positive regard for the school reading program and in their confidence that their children could succeed at difficult tasks. Dix (*11*) observed that parents of poor readers in grades one through six defined reading as word attack. Parents of good readers viewed reading more globally, as a source of knowledge, enjoyment, and adventure. (See, also, Chapter 1 of this volume.)
6. *Encourage parents to visit the classroom to observe reading instruction.* Prepare a videotape for parents unable to come during school hours. Take time to interpret aspects of the experience, answer questions, and suggest appropriate home follow-up activities.
7. *Arrange small group conferences for parents of children who have similar strengths and weaknesses.* Facilitate sharing of ideas for helping these children at home (*10*:709).
8. *Invite families to share in class functions that feature reading and books.* Present plays or puppet shows based on

favorite stories. Hold a book exchange for families of children in the class. Plan a project or hobby fair at which the reference books used are displayed along with the children's work.

9. *Maintain a resource room in the school for community use.* It might contain a library for parents, materials for game construction, and a meeting space for parents and teacher groups (22:713).

10. *Involve parents in curriculum decisions related to the language arts program.* Selecting library books, securing consumable materials, and setting up community outreach or volunteer tutor programs are tasks parents may undertake (22:712).

11. *Visit homes of families the school is not reaching.* Take a book or game that will enable you to model a strategy for helping the child at home. In some communities, supportive parents volunteer to call on and assist other families (35).

12. *Keep in regular contact with families through a bulletin or newsletter.* Periodical features might include booklists of family reading suggestions, seasonal ideas for reading-related activities, and announcements of community events that might foster language growth or family togetherness.

13. *Prepare booklets or calendars suggesting reading for use during vacations.*

14. *Remember that papers sent home with children communicate to adults in the home.* Show judicious praise, criticism, and appreciation in comments written on children's work. Guide parents in their treatment of homework through notes or telephone calls that clarify the purpose of certain assignments.

15. *Construct learning or activity packets for home use.* Design a rotating schedule that enables children to share the packets with their families. Make home learning kits from common materials so that parents can easily duplicate them or so you can replace them as necessary.

16. *Invite parents to make cassette tapes for classroom use.* Children enjoy hearing members of their families read stories or give directions at the listening station. Involve fathers as well as mothers in this endeavor.

17. *Be sensitive to the needs of parents as you support family involvement.* Nonreading parents may be particularly threatened by reading-related activities. Parents who have not built up patterns of communication with their children through the years may need very concrete support as they establish new patterns.

18. *Recognize the contributions of families to their children's reading and language growth.* This may be done formally through certificates or citations or informally as parents and teachers share their experiences.

19. *Seek community support in planning and funding projects that foster family involvement.* Libraries, service clubs, businesses, industries, government agencies, private foundations, and IRA councils stand ready to help teachers and parents forge partnerships for the reading success of children.

References

1. ANDERSON, L. A. "How to Read a Report on Reading in the Popular Press," in Carl B. Smith (Ed.), *Parents and Reading*. Newark, Delaware: International Reading Association, 1971.
2. ARBUTHNOT, M. H. *Children's Reading in the Home.* Glenview, Illinois: Scott, Foresman, 1969.
3. BERHRMANN, P. "Help for Home," *Grade Teacher*, 89 (1972), 16-18.
4. BREILING, A. "Using Parents as Teaching Partners," *Reading Teacher*, 30 (1976), 187-192.
5. CASSIDY, J. "Reporting Pupil Progress in Reading—Parents versus Teachers," *Reading Teacher*, 31 (1977), 294-296.
6. CASSIDY, J., and C. VUKELICH. "Survival Reading for Parents and Kids: A Parent Education Program," *Reading Teacher*, 31 (1978), 638-641.
7. CHAMBERS, A. "The Making of a Literary Reader," *Horn Book Magazine*, 51 (1975), 301-310.
8. CHAN, J.M.T. *Why Read Aloud to Children?* Newark, Delaware: International Reading Association, 1974.
9. COLE, A., and others. "Reaching Out to Parents," *Teacher*, 92 (1974), 120-121.
10. DAVIS, E.S. "Parents and Schools Should Share," *Reading Teacher*, 23 (1970), 707-710.
11. DIX, M. *Are Reading Habits of Parents Related to Reading Performance of Their Children?* Chicago: 1976. (ED 133 693)
12. DUNCAN, L. J., and B. VON BEHREN. "PEPPER—A Spicy New Reading Program," *Reading Teacher*, 27 (1974), 180-183.
13. FORGAN, H. W. *Help Your Child Learn to Read.* Toronto, Ontario: Pagurian Press, 1975.
14. FRESHOUR, F. W. "Beginning Reading: Parents Can Help," *Reading Teacher*, 25 (1972), 513-516.

15. GAGLIARDO, R. "What a Parent Can Do to Help In the Home," in Carl B. Smith (Ed.), *Parents and Reading*. Newark, Delaware: International Reading Association, 1971.

16. GALLUP, G. "Survey Shows Parents Willing to Help with Child's Education," *The Manhattan Mercury*, September 29, 1977, B5 (Manhattan, Kansas).

17. GEISTLINGER, L. J. "Dial-a-Story," in Ferne Johnson (Ed.), *Start Early for an Early Start*. Chicago: American Library Association, 1976.

18. GEORGE, J. E. "Correlates of Reading Deficiency: The Relationship of Preschool Experiences to Reading Achievement," University of Missouri at Kansas City, 1972. (ED 089 197)

13. GORDON, T. *P.E.T.: Parent Effectiveness Training*. New York: Peter H. Wyden, 1970.

20. GRANOWSKY, A., F. R. MIDDLETON, and J. MUMFORD. *For Parents and Children: A Guide for Better Reading*. Ashville, North Carolina: Tarmac, 1977.

21. GRANSTROM, J. "Families in Reading," in Ferne Johnson (Ed.), *Start Early for an Early Start*. Chicago: American Library Association, 1976.

22. HARRINGTON, A. "Parents and the School," *Reading Teacher*, 23 (1970), 711-716, 726.

23. HARRINGTON, A. "Teaching Parents to Help at Home," in Carl B. Smith (Ed.), *Parents and Reading*. Newark, Delaware: International Reading Association, 1971.

24. HOSKISSON, K. "Should Parents Teach Their Children to Read?" *Elementary English*, 51 (1974), 295-299.

25. HURWITZ, A., and A. GODDARD. *Games to Improve Your Child's English*. New York: Simon and Schuster, 1969.

26. JOHNSON, M. S. "Reading Readiness—What Parents Should Know about It," in Virginia H. Mathews (Ed.), *A Parent's Guide to Reading Instruction*. Harrisburg, Pennsylvania: Pennsylvania Department of Education, 1972.

27. KASDON, L. M. "Causes of Reading Difficulties," in Carl B. Smith (Ed.), *Parents and Reading*. Newark, Delaware: International Reading Association, 1971.

28. KLOEFKORN, M.B., and M.E.M. FANGO. *Parents, You Can Help!* International Reading Association, Colorado, Council, n.d.

29. KNOX, G. M. "Your Child Can't Read: How Can You Help?" *Better Homes and Gardens*, 1972, 4-8, 38-40.

30. LaCROSSE, E. R. "Getting Ready to Read," in Virginia H. Mathews (Ed.), *A Parent's Guide to Reading Instruction*. Harrisburg, Pennsylvania: Pennsylvania Department of Education, 1972.

31. LARRICK, N.A. *A Parent's Guide to Children's Reading*. Garden City, New Jersey: Doubleday, 1964.

32. LARRICK, N. "How to Help the Beginning Reader," *New York Times*, January 8, 1975, Ed5, SED.

33. MATHEWS, V. H. "Getting Help on Reading Outside of School," in Virginia H. Mathews (Ed.), *A Parent's Guide to Reading Instruction*. Harrisburg, Pennsylvania: Pennsylvania Department of Education, 1972.

34. McKEE, P. *Primer for Parents*. Boston, Massachusetts: Houghton Mifflin, 1975.

35. McWILLIAMS, D., and P. M. CUNNINGHAM. "Project PEP," *Reading Teacher*, 29 (1976), 653-655.

36. MERGENTIME, C. *You and Your Child's Reading: A Practical Guide for Parents*. New York: Harcourt Brace Jovanovich, 1962.

37. MILLER, B. "What Parents Can Do for the School," in Carl B. Smith (Ed.), *Parents and Reading.* Newark, Delaware: International Reading Association, 1971.
38. NEIDERMEYER, F. "Parents Teach Kindergarten Reading at Home," *Elementary School Journal,* 70 (1970), 438-445.
39. PEYSON, L. "The Possible Dream—Parents As Partners," presentation at the International Reading Association Sixth Plains Regional Conference, Kansas City, Missouri, 1978.
40. PIKULSKI, J. "Parents Can Aid Reading Growth," *Elementary English,* 51 (1974), 883-884.
41. RANSBURY, M. K. *How Can I Encourage My Primary Grade Child to Read?* Newark, Delaware: International Reading Association, 1972.
42. ROBERSON, D.R. "Parents and Teachers: Partners in the Teaching of Reading," *Reading Teacher,* 23 (1970), 772-726.
43. ROGERS, N. *How Can I Help My Child Get Ready to Read?* Newark, Delaware: International Reading Association, 1972.
44. ROSENQUIST, A. R. "School and Home Cooperation and the Reading Achievement of First Grade Pupils," doctoral dissertation, University of California at Berkeley, 1972. *Dissertation Abstracts International,* 1972, 6749-A. (University Microfilms, No. 72-18.045)
45. RUBIN, D., and E. SHROBE. *Your Child and Reading: How You Can Help.* Boston, Massachusetts: Houghton Mifflin, 1973.
46. SLOAN, G. D. *Good Books Make Reading Fun for Your Child.* IRA + Eric/ Crier, n.d.
47. SMITH, C. B. "The Effect of Environment on Learning to Read," in Carl B. Smith (Ed.), *Parents and Reading.* Newark, Delaware: International Reading Association, 1971.
48. STRANG, R. *Helping Your Child Improve His Reading.* New York: E. P. Dutton, 1962.
49. SULLIVAN, H. J., and C. LaBEAUNE. "Parents: Summer Reading Teachers," *Elementary School Journal,* 72 (1971), 279-285.
50. TINKER, M. G. *Preparing Your Child for Reading.* New York: Holt, Rinehart and Winston, 1971.
51. WAGNER, G., R. SCOTT, and J. CESINGER. *Home Start Ideabook.* Darien, Connecticut: Early Years Press, 1976.
52. WARTENBERG, A. "A Parent-Teacher Speaks," *Reading Teacher,* 23 (1970), 748-750.
53. WARTENBERG, H. "Parents in the Reading Program," *Reading Teacher,* 23 (1970), 717-721, 740.
54. WRIGHT, D. R., and others. *Your Child Learns through Discovery.* Boise, Idaho: Right to Read, State of Idaho Department of Public Education, n.d.

Continued Focus on Families for Cultural Appreciation, Curriculum Planning, and Tutoring in Reading

Mary J. Heimberger
Wardlaw College of Education
University of South Carolina
Columbia, South Carolina
United States of America

Betty Horodezky and Mary Harris have dealt with how parents can prepare for reading success during children's early years. As children acquire the experiences and oral language prerequisite for formal reading instruction, they absorb from the family settings and the parents vast amounts of information and strong feelings about their culture.

Cross-cultural studies in reading show that reading itself is valued differently in different cultures. For example, the American culture "values the skills of reading and writing highly indeed. The great majority of the world's research, scholarly articles and theoretical and professional books on the topic of reading comes from the United States" (7:347).

Cultural Heritage

The valuing of literacy is passed on to children by their parents. If parents highly value reading, they will instill a value for reading in their children, because parents are visible role models for children.

In a survey by Artley (1), students majoring in education were asked what turned them on or off about learning how to read. They were asked, "Was there someone or something besides your teachers who contributed to your competence and interest in reading?" Responses showed overwhelmingly that parents or family were a major influence. In most cases, the students cited parents who read to them when they were children. In some cases, the students recalled that they, themselves, had read to their parents or to other family members.

An interesting parent education program in which parent-child communication and the sharing of culture were emphasized is reported by Gollub (11). The program originated as a ten week course in which parents were given a homework assignment to do a series of short, daily activities with one or more of their children to increase family communication. These so-called Family Rituals were imaginative, amusing exercises to be done "at a special time and in a special place set apart from daily routines." Each ritual has three parts: a warm-up activity, a main activity, and a feedback method. See sample, "Song and Titles."

A total of fifty-six rituals have been developed, many of which emphasize the sharing and appreciation of one's culture. The rituals have been incorporated into a series of eight booklets distributed by the School District of Philadelphia, Pennsylvania. Several of the parents involved in this unique program began generating their own rituals after using the booklets.

Many less structured experiences involving culture are a part of children's upbringing. Storytelling, the passing on of family histories, and preparing for and celebrating special holidays and festivities (such as Russian Easter or the Cuban "Fiesta de Los Quince Ano") are examples of how families foster cultural appreciation in their children.

Reading aloud has been cited earlier as an example of a family activity that has great merit. Botel (2) includes this activity as one of four critical experiences that *both* home and school should provide for children. The other three experiences are sustained silent reading, composing (both oral and written), and investigating language patterns. Interestingly, these four critical experiences are the basis for the new Pennsylvania reading language arts curriculum. Botel suggests that all of these activities should be stressed daily at every level, in the home environment as well as in the classroom. He feels that good readers (and writers) become so because of a "literate

SONG AND TITLES
Warmup

Think of a song you both know the words to. Instead of singing it, say it together VERY DRAMATICALLY. Really ham it up—like Shakespeare or something like that.

Main Activity

Each of you list 5 songs you like. Write the names here.

Person 1   Person 2

1. _____   1. _____

2. _____   2. _____

3. _____   3. _____

4. _____   4. _____

5. _____   5. _____

Now, imagine that a show is being written about your family. It's your job to think of 10 song titles that could be in the show. The titles can be funny, they can be first lines of songs, etc. Work together and don't criticize each other's ideas.

1. _____

2. _____

3. _____

4. _____

5. _____

6. _____

7. _____

8. _____

9. _____

10. _____

Pick out your favorite title and see if you can write the first lines of the song   Title # _____

first two lines _____

_____

FEEDBACK:

How much fun was this? No fun at all 1 2 3 4 5 Heaps/Gobs/ Barrels

How hard was this?   Tough   1 2 3 4 5 A Snap

Write a song title that says how each of you feels about today's ritual.

Young Person's Title _____

Older Person's Title _____

environment": those conditions which provide the child with firsthand experiences with literacy and which are not bound by socioeconomic class or ethnic background.

Weiser (28) goes along with Botel in emphasizing the importance of parents' 1) serving as reading models, 2) reading to children, and 3) providing "experiences and explorations of language" in the home. In addition to these suggestions, Wartenberg (26) recommends that parents should provide a variety of reading materials for children, suggest appropriate entertainment, and encourage pets and hobbies.

Pikulski (19) expands on these informal suggestions for the home, gearing his recommendations to the parents of children with reading problems. Another useful source of ideas is a simple manual entitled "Your Child and Reading: How You Can Help," available from Houghton Mifflin (29).

Programs to Guide Tutoring at Home

There are also more formalized, school sponsored attempts to assist parents in helping their children in the home which are noteworthy. Harrington (14) set up an adult education program in Hamburg, New York, which featured class sessions centered on reading to provide helpful hints for skill development, to suggest activities, and to refer casually to some published materials available to parents. The specific program is detailed in her book *How to Help Your Child with Reading at Home*.

The Los Angeles, California, Unified School District Adult Division has developed lecture-discussion programs and television courses to help parents with their children's reading instruction. Tutorial reading clinics and handbooks for parents which suggest ideas for home use to accompany the school readers are made available. Seven types of adult courses involving different amounts of time, different levels, and different types of reading (developmental or remedial) are described (6).

The Montgomery County, Maryland, Public Schools' Title I Parents-in-Reading Program provided parents with books which were at the appropriate levels for their children, along with suggestions for exposing children to spoken and written language in new and interesting ways. Also, homemade reading games were made by parents in scheduled workshops. The Reading-at-Home segment of the program included home reading awards (homemade badges) or prizes from a treasure chest of donated materials. Parents were asked to certify in writing that their children had read for a stated amount of time at home. The program also provided a lending library of reading games, mainly commercial, for parents to borrow and home learning kits for parents unable to attend scheduled school workshops (3).

Similar to the home learning kits are "parent training packages"—self-contained, portable instructional systems which parents can use with children at home—as described by Stowitschek and Hofmeister (25). These packages cover developmental skills areas (for example, color recognition) and are designed to carry over into the home. PEPPER (Parent Education Program to Pep-Up Every Reader) sponsored by the Title I program in Springfield, Illinois (8) and Project Homereach of the Wilkinsburg, Pennsylvania, Public Schools (10) also employ school-prepared learning packets for home use by parents.

An at-home remedial reading program conducted with parental help is described by Fager and Williams (9). Parent meetings, handbooks giving background on specific reading skills, and suggested activities and ideas for motivation are all components of this program which is geared toward helping the child master reading difficulties outside of school. The Parent Education Program (PEP) of the Newark, Delaware, schools enables parents to teach survival skills such as reading road signs and menus by conducting workshops in which parents make games for teaching these skills (4).

Another remedial strategy, the Assisted Reading Technique, in which the child reads aloud and the parent supplies unknown words, is described in a study by Hoskissen, Sherman, and Smith (16). They demonstrated that parents can be quickly trained in Assisted Reading and thereafter can help disabled readers. They found that children feel better about reading and read more after the Assisted Reading approach was used.

The New Haven, Connecticut, Public Schools provide a final exemplary program involving some home tutoring by parents. Six varied activities for parent involvement are utilized (5):

1. Parent Reading Courses (all about the reading process and how to aid it at home).
2. Be My Guest Programs (parents visit the school reading program and discuss it with appropriate personnel).
3. Summer Reading Program (parents sign a Pledge of Active Support and encourage their child to enroll in the program, then take the child to the library and hold conferences about books read).
4. Book Bank (parents collect and distribute used books to children).
5. Reading Workshops for Parents ("make and take" reading games and distribution of a parent handbook with reading suggestions).
6. School Program (parents work as instructional aides and as community tutors outside of school, in both large and small group situations).

To summarize the importance of specific suggestions and programs to prepare parents for home tutoring, Artley recommends that "parents be made 'full-fledged partners in the educational process' through information on the school reading program and suggestions of supplemental home activities" (3:187).

Family Volunteers at School

When parents act as full-fledged partners, their involvement in reading tutoring can extend beyond the home into the classroom. Moms, and sometimes Dads, now may be found in school during the regular school day, and not just as invited spectators.

"Federal and local funds have made parent participation as paid teacher aides possible. A perhaps amazingly 'unrelated' and 'extraordinary' outgrowth of this has been the empirical evidence that many parents are willing to work for schools on a nonpaid basis, particularly in the reading area, and probably because it gives them an opportunity to learn what is happening . . . they can serve in valuable roles as aides and be very supportive of the program if they are trained and employed properly" (27:720).

There are certain pitfalls to be avoided when placing parent aides or volunteers in classrooms. It does not seem advisable to place parents in their child's class if the parents will be there much of the time. Some schools will not even place parents at the same grade levels as their own children, because of the problems caused by parents making comparisons. "Most important, parents should not be pulled into a program just for the sake of having parent involvement. If parents are to be effective, there must be some time spent in meaningful preparation" (27:721).

Parent volunteer training programs appear at both national and state levels in the United States. The National Reading Center has developed an extensive program which involves state workshops for tutor trainers who then go to individual locales to train parent volunteers (20). The Center recommends that the following points be considered in tutor training:

1. The design and implementation of adequate training programs to prepare tutors for their jobs.
2. Definition of the tutorial program so that it clearly outlines specific goals for children being tutored. This includes providing enough descriptive and/or diagnostic material for the tutor ahead of time so that teaching can be geared to these goals.
3. Provision for adequate supervision for the tutor.
4. Provision for formal evaluation of the child's progress at the end of a definitive time, for feedback as to tutoring efficacy.
5. Provision for a supervisor of the tutorial program.
6. Planning of specific space and materials for tutoring (20).

Some tasks which parents might undertake in the school's reading program are suggested below.

1. *Implementation of instruction*
   a. Provide practice experiences of many types for individual pupils or groups (flash card drills, comprehension checks, workbook assignments).

b. Provide individual assistance to pupils who need clarification of directions and other types of assistance as they work.
c. Read to pupils.
d. Monitor or supervise students engaged in an activity initiated by the teacher.
e. Assist pupils engaged in independent activities (learning packets, programed materials, etc.).

2. *Assessment of pupil progress*
a. Assist in monitoring test activities.
b. Render individual assistance to pupils with special needs during testing sessions.
c. Assist the teacher with the mechanics of scoring.
d. Record test results.
e. Compile lists of weaknesses as revealed by errors on tests. (Paraprofessionals and Reading Committee of the IRA, 1973, Special Insert)

Three good sources of information for planning and implementing parent tutoring programs in the schools are *Guidebook for the Volunteer Reading Teacher* by Lenore Sleisinger; *Handbook for the Volunteer Tutor*, compiled by Sidney J. Rauch; and *Parents: Active Partners in Education*, prepared by Mary Lou Sayler. The first two sources concentrate on specifics of the tutor's role, the third is a comprehensive guide to setting up a parent involvement program in a community or school district.

Exemplary Volunteer Programs

A few specific examples of good public school programs should be pointed out here. The Houston Independent School District in Houston, Texas, has had its VIPS (Volunteers in Public Schools) Program since 1970. Parents can enlist in any one of a number of voluntary tutoring projects, ranging in subjects from reading to motor skills (mini-gym) to art enrichment. The basic purpose behind VIPS is "the improvement of the adult-child ratio so that those who need help receive more individualized instruction" (*17*:57-58).

The Houston program begins with a solid orientation. "There is on site basic training in school policies and procedures, then the development of special interest groups for more specific training" (17:59). The entire program is thoroughly explained in the Handbook for Volunteers in Public Schools, available from the Houston Independent School District, 3830 Richmond Avenue, Houston, Texas 77027, USA.

The Spencerport, New York, Central Schools began a parent aide program in 1968 with 25 volunteers. It expanded to 521 volunteers during the 1977-1978 school year, during which a total of 30,269 hours of time was volunteered. Some parents are recruited through a letter that is sent home via children in all district buildings. Others are recommended by teachers who know them and highly support their recruitment. There is a week of general orientation (usually one of the first weeks of school, in either the mornings or the afternoons) after which more specific training is left to the individual teachers to whom the parent aides are assigned. Those aides, who work heavily in tutoring reading, also attend special workshops coordinated by Title I reading personnel. Topics such as reading terminology, grouping, methods, and materials for reading instruction are covered. Workshops for making reading materials and activities are provided, also.

Not all parents work in an instructional capacity. Some prefer to do noninstructional tasks such as marking papers and recording grades or test results, running stencils, or doing other clerical duties. A few volunteers do a combination of instructional and noninstructional work. Many parents volunteer to be available as school resource persons in various areas such as crafts, travel, and local history. Some volunteers even babysit in their own homes so that other volunteers can spend their time in the schools.

The Spencerport program has complete support from the Board of Education and the school administration. A full-time aide coordinator administers the program. There is a high degree of flexibility and communication among regular school personnel and the volunteers in Spencerport. Many parents have been involved since the program's inception; some have been motivated by their participation to go back to college and earn teacher certification (15).

A parent volunteer program that began in 1973 in Mount Clemens, Michigan, has "Reading Moms" assigned to remedial students. Unlike most other volunteer tutor programs, there is no required training. The Reading Moms "should be ready listeners and trustworthy confidants" to support the students and make them more comfortable about reading. The tutor role is largely an affective one, less related to skill development than in most programs (23:498).

The programs described are but a sampling of the many parent volunteer programs proliferating all over the United States. Two other projects worthy of mention in this regard are the School Volunteer Development Project of Dade County, Florida, and PQRST, a newly developed special interest group of the International Reading Association.

The School Volunteer Development Project is a federally funded program which has been developed by the Dade County Public Schools in Miami, Florida. This program makes available training materials for school volunteers—kits, handbooks, training modules, and films. Some of the sample materials are titled "Becoming a School Volunteer," "Assisting in the Classroom," "Building One-to-One Relationships," "Training for Reading Tutors," and "How to Listen to Children." The first four are handbooks and modules, the last is a film. Additional information and order forms for materials are available from the School Volunteer Development Project, 1410 N.E. Second Avenue, Miami, Florida 33132, USA.

PQRST is an acronym for Parents for Quality Reading for Students and Teachers. Its purpose is fourfold:

1. To support programing in reading that involves parents in the instructional process;
2. to support national, state, and local reading councils in the organization and development of parent affiliates;
3. to involve parents in the development of a legislative support system for reading instruction; and
4. to publish a newsletter dealing with parents and reading.

The Michigan Reading Association of IRA has promoted this new special interest group. Its organizational meeting was held at the International Reading Association Convention in Houston.

Obviously, there are many educational programs featuring tutoring and other forms of parental involvement in reading in the public schools. This movement should lead further to the natural involvement of parents in planning the school curriculum. Generally, parents are informed about the curriculum, but may have little or no say about its composition and development.

According to Goulet (13:163), "Parents have begun to play a more instrumental role in determining early childhood curricula." In a study of kindergarten curricula, Goulet found that parents agreed in ranking the importance of developmental domains (i.e., physical, social, self-concept, sensory, perceptual, emotional, language, academic) as to their importance in kindergarten. He concluded that "divergent group concerns must be considered." It remains to be seen whether growing parent involvement and influence in the schools will affect the development of new and better reading curricula.

Most authorities say that the education of children should be regarded as a team project for both home and school. As partners in the reading program, "parents are often in a better position to discover children's interests and to perceive children's emotional reactions toward the reading situation. [They] can provide them an abundance of love and encouragement, a great variety of play, creative and constructive expeiences, and unlimited opportunity for free reading in good books and magazines" (12:918). Educators need to encourage parents not only to provide rich language development experiences at home, but also to reap the pleasure of serving as parent volunteers and resource persons at the school.

In recent decades, the explosion of knowledge has combined with the explosion of population in the developing countries to make the problems of universal education almost insurmountable. If families can be encouraged to support school literacy efforts vigorously, however, they can produce activity in reading that will ignite renewed fires of learning.

References

1. ARTLEY, A. STERL. "Good Teachers of Reading: Who Are They?" *Reading Teacher*, 29 (October 1975), 26-31.

2. BOTEL, MORTON. "Making Reading Public," address to the Rochester Area Reading Council of the International Reading Association, May 1978.
3. BREILING, ANNETTE. "Using Parents as Teaching Partners," *Reading Teacher*, 30 (November 1976), 187-192.
4. CASSIDY, JACK, and CAROL VUKELICH. "Survival Reading for Parents and Kids: A Parent Education Program," *Reading Teacher*, 31 (March 1978), 638-641.
5. CRISCUOLO, NICHOLAS P. "Parents: Active Partners in the Reading Process," *Elementary English*, 51 (September 1974), 883-884.
6. DeFRANCO, ELLEN B. "Parent Education as an Aid to Improving Children's Reading," *Adult Leadership*, 21 (April 1973), 320-323.
7. DOWNING, JOHN. "Cultural Priorities and the Acquisition of Literacy," *International Review of Education*, 19 (1973), 345-355.
8. DUNCAN, LINDA, and BARBARA VON BEHREN. "Pepper—A Spicy New Program," *Reading Teacher*, 28 (November 1974), 180-183.
9. FAGER, MARTHA, and LEONARD WILLIAMS. "Wanted: Parents Involved in Remedial Reading Programs," *School and Community*, 59 (January 1973), 27.
10. FLEMING, BETTY. "Reading Resource Teacher in the Wilkinsburg, Pennsylvania, Public Schools," interview, May 1978.
11. GOLLUB, WENDY. "Family Communication Rituals to Aid Children's Learning," *Language Arts*, 54 (September 1977), 655-660.
12. GOODMAN, SHIRLEY. "Parents as Partners in Our Reading Program," *Reading Teacher*, 30 (May 1977), 918.
13. GOULET, JOHN E. "Curriculum Priorities of Teachers and Parents in the Kindergarten Classroom," *Reading Improvement*, 12 (Fall 1975), 163-167.
14. HARRINGTON, ALMA. "Teaching Parents to Help at Home," in Carl B. Smith (Ed.), *Parents and Reading*. Newark, Delaware: International Reading Association, 1971.
15. HEFKE, JEAN, and PAT DENNIS. Interview, May 1978.
16. HOSKISSEN, KENNETH, THOMAS SHERMAN, and LINDA SMITH. "Assisted Reading and Parent Involvement," *Reading Teacher*, 27 (October 1974), 710-714.
17. MASSEY, JAMES H., and JEAN DAVIS MYERS. "Volunteer Mothers as Tutors in the Classroom," *Journal of Research and Development in Education*, 8 (Winter 1975), 54-63.
18. Paraprofessionals and Reading Committee of the International Reading Association. "Paraprofessionals and Reading," *Reading Teacher*, 27 (December 1973), special insert after page 336.
19. PIKULSKI, JOHN. "Parents Can Aid Reading Growth," *Elementary English*, 51 (September 1974), 896-897.
20. RAIM, JOAN. "Rolling Out the Welcome Mat to Tutors," *Reading Teacher*, 26 (April 1973), 696-701.
21. RAUCH, SIDNEY (Ed.). *Handbook for the Volunteer Tutor*. Newark, Delaware: International Reading Association, 1969.
22. SAYLER, MARY LOU. *Parents: Active Partners in Education*. Washington, D.C.: American Association of Elementary-Kindergarten-Nursery Education, National Education Association, 1971.
23. SCULLEN, T., and D. CURD. "Reading Moms: A Program that Works," *Phi Delta Kappan*, 58 (February 1977), 498-499.
24. SLEISINGER, LENORE. *Guidebook for the Volunteer Reading Teacher*. New York: Teachers College Press, Columbia University, 1965.

25. STOWITSCHEK, JOSEPH J., and ALAN HOFMEISTER. "Parent Training Packages," *Children Today*, March/April 1975, 23-25.
26. WARTENBERG, ARLENE. "A Parent-Teacher Speaks," *Reading Teacher*, 23 (May 1970), 748-750.
27. WARTENBERG, HERBERT. "Parents in the Reading Program," *Reading Teacher*, 23 (May 1970), 717-721.
28. WEISER, M. H. "Parental Responsibility in the Teaching of Reading," *Young Children*, 29 (May 1974), 225-230.
29. *Your Child and Reading: How You Can Help*. Boston: Houghton Mifflin, 1973.